CHRIST THE ETERNAL SON

Christ
the Eternal Son

A.W. Tozer

Edited and Compiled by Gerald B. Smith

WingSpread Publishers
Camp Hill, Pennsylvania

WingSpread Publishers

Camp Hill, Pennsylvania
www.wingspreadpublishers.com

A division of Zur Ltd.

Christ the Eternal Son
ISBN: 978-1-60066-047-4
© 1982, 1992 by Zur Ltd.

Previously published by Christian Publications, Inc.
First Christian Publications Edition 1982
First WingSpread Publishers Edition 2010

Scripture taken from
the Holy Bible: King James Version

CONTENTS

Preface

If Dr. A.W. Tozer ever became impatient with his fellow Christians during his lifetime, it was because they showed too little inclination to think and to ponder and to meditate on eternity!

In the sermon which constitutes the first chapter of this book, Dr. Tozer was apparently chiding his hearers when he said: "If you do not engage in deep thinking, it may not seem so amazing, but if you have given yourself to frequent thoughtful consideration, you are astonished at the bridging of the great gulf between God and not God."

Later, he spoke of his own practice of thoughtful meditation when he said: "I admit that I like to dream and dwell in my thoughts upon those ages long past."

In the third chapter, speaking of sensitivity to divine truth, Dr. Tozer said: "We must meditate on the eternal nature of God in order to worship as we should."

Then he added, openly chiding this time: "Now, if you have one of those mousetrap minds, open and shut, you will casually remark: 'It is all quite simple—that is the attribute of God called eternity. You will find it in a footnote on page 71 in So and So's Systematic Theology. Now, let's go out and have a soda.'"

In these chapters you will also find Dr. Tozer's confession of his basic "spiritual philosophy." Simply, it was this: "Everything is wrong until Jesus sets it right!"

Introduction

Thoughts on the Mysticism of John, the Apostle

I believe I had anticipated that it was going to be a pleasure to expound this beautiful and high-soaring Gospel of John. However, I must confess that in my preparation and study a sense of inadequacy has come over me—a feeling of inadequacy so stunning, so almost paralyzing that I am not at this juncture able to call it a pleasure to preach.

Perhaps this will be God's way of reducing the flesh to a minimum and giving the Holy Spirit the best possible opportunity to do His eternal work. I fear that sometimes our own eloquence and our own concepts may get in the way, for the unlimited ability to talk endlessly about religion is a questionable blessing.

One of the great Bible expositors of the past, A. T. Robertson, has given us this brief assessment of the Gospel of John:

"The test of time has given the palm to the fourth Gospel over all the books of the world. If Luke's Gospel is the most beautiful, John's Gospel is supreme in its height and depth and reach of thought.

"The picture of Christ here given is the one that has captured the mind and heart of mankind. The language of this Gospel has the clarity of a spring, but we are not able to sound the depths of the bottom of it. Lucidity and profundity—that is, it is so clear that you can see through it; but so deep that you cannot see clear through it."

I think that is wonderfully stated.

Now, this John who has given us this Gospel is surely the mystic of the New Testament. I started to say that this John *was* the mystic of the New Testament—but we must be very careful not to put a *was* where God put an *is* for there are no past tenses with the children of God.

Jesus argued for immortality on the grounds that God is not the God of the dead, but of the living, for the dead are past.

When we talk about a dead man we say *was*, but when we talk about a living man, we say *is*. Therefore, it is not really theologically proper to say that John was the mystic of the New Testament. We say, rather, that John is the mystic of the New Testament, even as Paul is the theologian of the New Testament.

Now, this naturally brings together two closely related words: *mysticism* and *theology*. I mention these words here because in the minds of some people there is an idea that there is a contradiction between mysticism and theology, between the mystic and the theologian.

Somehow the mystic has earned himself a doubtful reputation, or rather, he has had a doubtful reputation earned for him. That is why so many people feel that they must shy away from anyone who is said to be a mystic.

But John is the mystic of the New Testament even as Paul is the theologian—and I want you to know and understand that in Paul's theology there is much mysticism and in John's mysticism there is much theology.

So, in acknowledging that, we do not have a contradiction. We have the one complementing and supplementing the other.

The man Paul possessed an unusual intellect and God was able to pour into his great mind and spirit the great basic doctrines of the New Testament. For God's purposes Paul was able then to think them through and reason them out and set them down logically; thus he holds that reputation as theologian.

But in the mind of John, God found something different altogether—He found a harp that wanted to sit in the window and catch the wind. He found that John had a birdlike sense about him that wanted to take flight all the time.

Thus, God allowed John, starting from the same premises as the theologian Paul, to mount and soar and sing.

Shakespeare in one of his sonnets drew this word picture:

Like to the lark at break of day,
Arising from sullen earth
Sings hymns at heaven's gate.

Some may read this Gospel and then say, "John was"—but John *is*, still is like the lark that rises at the break of day and shakes the dew of the night from his wings and soars to heaven's gate, singing, singing. He does not really soar any higher than Paul, but he sings just a little bit sweeter and thus gets our rapt attention a little more quickly.

So, in the New Testament, Paul is the theologian who lays foundations strong, and John gets on the parapet, flaps his wings and takes off. That is why it is difficult to preach from John's heights.

Paul and John do not contradict one another; they do not cancel each other out. They complement each other in such a way that we may describe it by saying that Paul is the instrument and John is the music the instrument brings.

John gives us a beautiful portrait of the eternal Christ, starting with those stark words. *In the beginning*... And that is where we start with Christianity: not with Buddha and not with Mohammed; not with Joseph A. Smith and not with Mrs. Mary Baker Eddy; not with Father Divine and not with Madame Lavasky. All of these and the countless others like them had a beginning and they all had an ending.

But our Christian life commences with Him who had no beginning and never can have any ending, namely, the Word who was with the Father in the beginning, the Word who was God and the Word who is God!

—A. W. Tozer

Great is the Mystery

And the Word was made flesh, and dwelt among us. . . . (John 1:14)

None of us can approach a serious study and consideration of the eternal nature and person of Jesus Christ without sensing and confessing our complete inadequacy in the face of the divine revelation.

Long ago the writer Milton had the courage and the imagination to select "Paradise Lost and Paradise Regained" for the theme of his great literary work, detailing the full sweep from the dim dawn of empty nothingness through to the triumph of Christ following his resurrection.

Milton said when he began his work that he was going to soar "above the Aeonian mount and justify the ways of God to men." When we read

Milton's literature we are astonished that he accomplished so much of what he set out to do.

A literary critic, in comparing Milton and Shakespeare, once commented that Shakespeare's imagination and brilliance of mind were so much greater than Milton's that he limited himself to small subjects and short sections of history. It was the view of the critic that if Shakespeare had attempted anything as vast as Milton's work, he would have died of plethora of thought—that the vastness of it would have called so much out of the man that his mind would have exploded.

That was one man's opinion and I introduce it only because of the feeling of inadequacy we sense even in our mild attempts to discover and expound the eternal truths we find within God's revelation to man.

Think of where the Apostle John leads us, taking us up and into the Godhead where no Milton could go and certainly no secular Shakespeare could ever go. John introduces us to spheres and circles of deity so high and lofty and noble that if we follow him, we will certainly die in the attempt.

What should we do, then?

All we can hope to do is to toddle along on our short legs and gaze heavenward, like a goose whose wings have been clipped but whose heart is in the sky. Those wings just will not take her there.

Now, I have said all of this because my best faith and my loftiest expectation do not allow me to believe that I can do justice to a text that begins: "And the Word was made flesh, and dwelt among us" (John 1:14) and concludes: "No man hath seen God at any time; the only begotten Son, which is in the bosom of the Father, he hath declared him" (18).

This is what we will attempt to do: we will walk along the broad seashore of God and pick up a shell here and a shell there, holding each up to the light to admire its beauty. While we may ultimately have a small store of shells to take with us, they can but remind us of the truth and the fact that there stretches the vastness of the seashore around the great lips of the oceans—and that still buried there is far more than we can ever hope to find or see!

Yes, we are told that *the Word was made flesh.* May I point out that within the statement of these few simple words is one of the deepest mysteries of human thought.

Thoughtful men are quick to ask: "How could the deity cross the wide, yawning gulf that separates what is God from that which is not God?" Perhaps you confess with me that in the universe there are really only two things, God and not God—that which is God and that which is not God.

No one could have made God, but God, the Creator, has made all of those things in the universe which are not God.

So, the gulf that separates the Creator and the creature, the gulf between the being we call God and all other beings, is a great and vast and yawning gulf.

Bridging the gulf

How God could bridge this great gulf is indeed one of the most profound and darkest mysteries to which human thought can be directed.

How is it possible that God could join the Creator to the creature?

If you do not engage in deep thinking, it may not seem so amazing, but if you have given yourself to frequent thoughtful consideration, you are astonished at the bridging of the great gulf between God and not God.

Let us be reminded that the very archangels and the seraphim and the cherubim who shield the stones of fire are not God.

We read our Bibles and discover that man is not the only order of beings. Man in his sinful pride, however, chooses to believe that he is the only such order.

Some Christian people and mankind in general foolishly refuse to believe in the reality of angelic beings. I have talked with enough people to have the feeling that they think of angels as Santa Clauses with wings!

Many say they do not believe in created orders of cherubim and seraphim or watchers or holy ones, or in any of the strange principalities and powers that walk so mysteriously and brightly through the passages of the Bible. Generally speaking, we do not believe in them as much as we should, at any rate.

We may not believe in them, brethren, but they are there!

Mankind is only one order of God's beings or creatures. So, we wonder: "How could the Infinite ever become finite? And how could the Limitless One deliberately impose limitations upon Himself? Why should God favor one order of beings above another in His revelation?"

In the book of Hebrews we learn to our amazement that God took not upon Him the nature of angels, but He took upon Him the seed of Abraham.

Now, Abraham certainly was not equal to an angel.

We would suppose that God in stepping down would step down just as little as possible. We would think that He would stop with the angels or the seraphim—but instead He came down to the lowest order and took upon Himself the nature of Abraham, the seed of Abraham.

The Apostle Paul throws up his hands in wonder at this point. Paul, declared to be one of the six great intellects of all time, throws up his hands and declares that "great is the mystery of godliness" (1 Timothy 3:16), the mystery of God manifest in the flesh.

Perhaps this is the most becoming approach to the subject for all of us: to just throw up our hands and say, "O Lord, you alone know!" There are so many more things in heaven and earth than are known in our theology—so it is in the deepest sense all mystery.

I would like to quote the gist of what John Wesley said concerning the eternal, mysterious act of God in stooping down to tabernacle with men.

Wesley declared that we should distinguish the act from the method by which the act is performed and advised that we do not reject a fact because we do not know how it was done. I think that is very wise!

I think also that it is very becoming for us to enter into the presence of God reverently, bowing our heads and singing His praises, and acknowledging His loving acts on our behalf even with our words, "It is true, O God, even if we do not know or understand how You have brought it all to pass!"

We will not reject the fact because we do not know the operation that brought it into being.

How much, then, can we know of this great mystery?

We can surely know this, at least: that the Incarnation required no compromise of deity. Let us always remember that when God became incarnate there was no compromise on God's part.

In times past, the mythical gods of the nations were no strangers to compromise. The Roman gods, the gods of the Grecian and Scandinavian legends, were gods that could easily compromise themselves and often did in the tales of mythical lore.

Never compromise

But the holy God who is God, and all else not God, our Father who art in heaven, could never compromise Himself. The Incarnation, the Word made flesh, was accomplished without any compromise of the holy Deity.

The living God did not degrade Himself by this condescension. He did not in any sense make Himself to be less than God.

He remained ever God and everything else remained not God. The gulf still existed even after Jesus Christ had become man and had dwelt among us. Instead of God degrading Himself when He became man, by the act of Incarnation He elevated mankind to Himself.

It is plain in the Athanasian Creed that the early church fathers were cautious at this point of doctrine. They would not allow us to believe that God, in the Incarnation, became flesh by a coming down of the Deity into flesh; but rather by the taking up of mankind into God.

Thus, we do not degrade God but we elevate man—and that is the wonder of redemption!

Then, too, there is another thing that we can know for sure about the acts of God—and that is that God can never back out of His bargain. This union of man with God is effected unto perpetuity!

In the sense which we have been considering, God can never cease to be man, for the second Person of the Trinity can never un-incarnate Himself, or de-incarnate Himself. The Incarnation remains forever a fact, for "And the Word was made flesh, and dwelt among us" (John 1:14).

We ought to turn our thoughts here to those earlier days in man's history, for after God had created Adam we know that the Creator communed with men.

I have leafed through a book entitled *Earth's Earliest Ages*. I will not say that I have actually read it because I quickly concluded that the author seems to believe that he knows more about the antediluvian period than Moses did. When I discover a man who claims to know more than Moses on a subject in which Moses is a specialist, I shy away from his book.

I admit that I like to dream and dwell in my thoughts upon those ages long past. I have always been fascinated by the Genesis passage which tells us that God came and walked in the garden in the cool of the day, calling for Adam. But Adam was not there.

I do not think we are reading anything into the account by assuming that God's meeting with Adam in this way was a common custom at that time. We are not told that this was the first time that God had come to take a walk with Adam in the midst of bird song and in the fading light.

God and man walked together and because the Creator had made man in His own image there was no degradation in His communion with man.

But now Adam is in hiding. Pride and disobedience, doubt and failure in testing—sin has broken off the communion and fellowship of the Creator with the created. The holy God must reject the fallen man, sending him from the garden and setting up a flaming sword that he might not return.

Lost the presence

Adam had lost the presence of the Creator God and in the Bible record of the ages that followed, God never dwelt with men again in quite the same way.

To the Israelites, God dwelt in the Shekinah, hidden in the fire and the cloud. Occasionally He would appear in what theologians call a theophany, an appearance of the Deity. God might speak briefly with a man as He did with Abraham in the tent door or with Gideon on the threshing floor. God did not linger; His appearance always cautious and veiled.

Even when God showed Himself to Moses it was in the fire of the burning bush or while Moses was hidden in the cleft of the rock. The eyes of fallen, sinful men were no longer able to endure the radiant majesty and glory of deity.

Then, in the fullness of time, He came again to men, for "And the Word was made flesh, and dwelt among us."

They called His name Immanuel, which means God with us. In that first coming of Jesus the Christ, God again came to dwell with men in person.

I will have you know that I am not a prepositional preacher but at this point we must note three prepositions having to do with the coming of Jesus, God appearing as man.

He appeared to dwell *with* men. He appeared to be united *to* men. He came to ultimately dwell *in* men forever. So, it is with men, and to men and in men that He came to dwell.

I always note with a little chuckle the frustrations of the translators when they come to such passages as "No man hath seen God at any time, the only begotten Son, which is in the bosom of the Father, he hath declared him" (John 1:18).

God's Word is just too big for the translators. They come to this phrase in the Greek: *The Son hath declared Him.* In the English of the King James Version it is just *declared.* In other versions they skirt it, they go around it, they plunge through it. They use two or three words and then they come back to one. They do everything to try to say what the Holy Ghost said, but they have to give up. Our English just will not say it all.

When we have used up our words and synonyms, we still have not said all that God revealed when He said: Nobody has ever seen God, but when Jesus Christ came He showed us what God is like (paraphrase of John 1:18).

I suppose that our simple and everyday language is as good as any.

"He has revealed Him—He has shown us what God is like!"

He has declared Him. He has set Him forth. He has revealed Him. In these ways the translators shift their language trying to get at this wondrous miracle of meaning.

But that man walking in Galilee was God acting like God. It was God, limited deliberately, having crossed the wide, mysterious gulf between God and not God; God and creature. No man had seen God at any time.

"The only begotten Son, which is in the bosom of the Father . . ." (John 1:18)—will you note that *was* is not the tense? Neither does it say that the Son *will be* in the Father's bosom. He *is* in the Father's bosom. It is stated in present, perpetual tense; the continuous tense, I think the grammarians call it. It is the language of continuation.

Therefore, when Jesus hung on the cross He did not leave the bosom of the Father.

You ask me, then: "Mr. Tozer, if that is true, why did our Lord Jesus cry out, 'My God, my God, why hast thou forsaken me?' " (Mark 15:34).

Was He frightened? Was He mistaken?

Never, never!

The answer should be very plain to us who love Him and serve Him.

Godhead never divided

Even when Christ Jesus died on that unholy, fly-infested cross for mankind, He never divided the Godhead. As the old theologians pointed out, you cannot divide the substance. Not all of Nero's swords could ever cut down through the substance of the Godhead to cut off the Father from the Son.

It was Mary's son who cried out, "Why hast thou forsaken me?"

It was the human body which God had given Him.

It was the sacrifice that cried, the lamb about to die.

It was the human Jesus. It was the Son of Man who cried.

Believe it that the ancient and timeless Deity was never separated; He was still in the bosom of the Father when He cried, "Into thy hands I commend my spirit" (Luke 23:46).

So the cross did not divide the Godhead—nothing can ever do that. One forever, indivisible, the substance undivided, three persons unconfounded.

Oh, the wonder of the ancient theology of the Christian Church! How little we know of it in our day of lightminded shallowness. How much we ought to know of it.

"No man hath seen God at any time, the only begotten Son, which is in the bosom of the Father, he hath declared him" (John 1:18).

God Manifest in the Flesh

And the Word was made flesh, and dwelt among us, (and we beheld his glory . . .), full of grace and truth. (John 1:14)

Many years ago Alexander Patterson wrote a great and compelling book titled *The Greater Life and Work of Christ*. I think it has been out of print for some years but it deserves to be reprinted. In his volume, this great preacher attempts to go back into the basic foundation of things and to encourage Christians to believe and trust and exalt Jesus Christ for being much more than the Redeemer of mankind.

I agree with him completely that Christ Jesus is not only Redeemer, but the Sustainer, the Creator, the Upholder, the One who holds all things together, the adhesive quality of the universe. To those who believe, Christ Jesus is the medium through whom God dispenses grace to all of His creatures, including those to be redeemed and those who do not need to be redeemed.

It is true that there are orders upon orders and ranks upon ranks of creatures that do not need to be redeemed. Yet, it is also true, that they live by grace as well as the lowest sinner who is converted.

Through the Apostle John, the Holy Spirit tells us that the eternal Son, the Word who became flesh, is full of grace and truth.

Everything by grace

Let us remember this: everything God does is by grace, for no man, no creature, no being deserves anything. Salvation is by grace, the Creation is by grace—all that God does is by grace and every human being has received of His fullness.

This boundless grace must operate wherever that which is not God appeals to that which is God; wherever the voice of the creature crosses the vast gulf to the ears of the Creator.

How do the angels get their broad wings?

Out of His grace.

How do the principalities and powers, the ranks and the columns of shining creatures appearing through the pages of the Bible get what they have?

Out of His grace upon grace.

I dare to ask in this context: What have you received of His grace and mercy?

Even though you may still be unconverted and going your own way, you have received much out of the ocean of His fullness. You have received the pulsing life that beats in your bosom. You have received the brilliant mind and brain within the protective covering of your skull. You have received a memory that strings the events you cherish and love as a jeweler strings pearls into a necklace and keeps them for you as long as you live and beyond.

All that you have is out of His grace. Jesus Christ, the eternal Word, who became flesh and dwelt among us, is the open channel through which God moves to provide all the benefits He gives to saints and sinners.

And what about the years, the rest of your existence?

You cannot believe that you have earned it.

You cannot believe that it has something to do with whether you are good or bad.

Confess that it is out of His grace, for the entire universe is the beneficiary of God's grace and goodness.

In the fifth chapter of Revelation, John bears record of the whole universe joining to give praise to the Lamb that was slain. Under the earth and on the earth and above the earth, John heard creatures praising Jesus Christ, all joining in a great chorus and

> Saying with a loud voice, Worthy is the Lamb
> that was slain to receive power, and riches,
> and wisdom, and strength, and honour, and

glory, and blessing, And every creature which is in heaven, and on the earth, and under the earth, and such as are in the sea, and all that are in them, heard I saying, Blessing, and honour, and glory, and power, be unto him that sitteth upon the throne, and unto the Lamb for ever and ever. (5:12–13).

Yes, surely the entire universe is a beneficiary of God's rich grace in Jesus Christ.

When we faithfully witness and present Christ to men and women in our day as Lord and Savior, we should remember that they are already receiving benefits of grace, and we are only presenting Jesus Christ to them in a new office—that of Redeemer.

When we say to an unbelieving man, *Believe on the Lord Jesus Christ,* we are actually saying to him: "Believe on the One who sustains you and upholds you and Who has given you life. Believe on the One who pities you and spares you and keeps you. Believe on the One out of whom you came!"

Never anything apart from Jesus

It is the truth that God has never done anything apart from Jesus Christ. The stars in their courses, the frogs that croak beside the lake, the angels in heaven above and men on earth below all came out of the channel we call the eternal Word. While we are busy presenting Jesus as Lord and Savior, it is true that we have all received out of His fullness.

Now, some time ago I wrote in an editorial concerning Jesus Christ that there can be no Saviorhood without Lordship. This was not original with me because I believe that the Bible plainly teaches that Jesus Christ is both Lord and Savior; that He is Lord before He is Savior; and that if He is not Lord, He is not Savior.

I repeat: when we present this Word, this eternal Word who was made flesh to dwell among us, as Lord and Savior, we present Him also in His other offices—Creator, Sustainer, and Benefactor.

It is the same Lord Jesus—and of Him John gives the faithful record: "Grace and truth came by Jesus Christ" (John 1:17).

I guess we all agree that the Law was given by Moses, and at this point I am not employing any contrast between Old and New Testaments. Any theological position that pits one Testament of the Bible against the other must come from a false theory.

The idea that the Old Testament is a book of law and the New Testament a book of grace is based on a completely false theory.

There is certainly as much about grace and mercy and love in the Old Testament as there is in the New. There is more about hell, more about judgment and the fury of God burning with fire upon sinful men in the New Testament than in the Old.

If you want excoriating, flagellating language that skins and blisters and burns, do not go back to Jeremiah and the old prophets—hear the words of Jesus Christ!

Oh, how often do we need to say it: the God of the Old Testament is the God of the New Testament. The Father in the Old Testament is the Father in the New Testament.

Furthermore, the Christ who was made flesh to dwell among us is the Christ who walked through all of the pages of the Old Testament.

Was it the law that forgave David when he had committed his great sins?

No, it was grace displayed in the Old Testament.

Was it grace that said, Babylon is fallen, the great harlot is fallen, Babylon is fallen? (paraphrase of Revelation 18:2).

No, it was law expressed in the New Testament.

Surely there is not this great difference and contrast between Old and New Testaments that many seem to assume. God never pits the Father against the Son. He never pits the Old Testament against the New.

The only contrast here is between all that Moses could do and all that Jesus Christ can do. The Law was given by Moses—that was all that Moses could do. Moses was not the channel through which God dispensed His grace.

God chose His only begotten Son as the channel for His grace and truth, for John witnesses that grace and truth came by Jesus Christ.

All that Moses could do was to command righteousness.

In contrast, only Jesus Christ produces righteousness.

All that Moses could do was to forbid us to sin.

In contrast, Jesus Christ came to save us from sin.

Moses could not save but Jesus Christ is both Lord and Savior.

Grace came through Jesus Christ before Mary wept in the manger stall in Bethlehem.

It was the grace of God in Christ that saved the human race from extinction when our first parents sinned in the garden.

It was the grace of God in Jesus Christ yet to be born that saved the eight persons when the Flood covered the earth.

It was the grace of God in Jesus Christ yet to be born but existing in preincarnation glory that forgave David when he sinned, that forgave Abraham when he lied. It was the grace of God that enabled Abraham to pray God down to ten when He was threatening to destroy Sodom.

God forgave Israel time and time again. It was the grace of God in Christ prior to the Incarnation that made God say, "I have risen early in the morning and stretched out my hands unto you!"

The Apostle John speaks for all of us also when he writes of the eternal Son and reminds us that *we beheld his glory.*

It is right that we should inquire, "What was this glory? Was it the glory of His works?"

Jesus was not only a worker—He was a wonder worker!

Every part of nature had to yield to Him and His authority.

He turned the water into wine and many people miss the point of His power and authority and argue about the difference between grape juice and wine. It mattered little—He turned water into wine. It was a miracle.

When our Lord came to the sick, He healed them. When He came to the devil-possessed, He commanded the devils to go out. When our Lord stood on the rocking deck of a tiny boat tossed by fierce winds and giant waves, He spoke to the water and rebuked the wind and there came a great calm.

Everything our Lord did was meaningful in the display of His eternal glory.

Think of the tenderness and compassion of the Lord Jesus when He raised the boy and gave him back to his widowed mother en route to the graveyard.

Think of the glory in His tenderness when He raised the little daughter of Jairus and restored her to her father's love and care.

I think Jesus probably smiled at that little girl after calling her back from her death sleep and said, "Sit up, daughter. Time to go to school."

You called your children when it was school time. I am sure Jesus used the same simple language of tenderness.

The works of our Lord were always dramatic works. Always they were amazing works. We wonder if John had these things in mind when he said, *We beheld his glory,* but I think not. I think John had a much greater glory in mind.

We can never know all of the wonderful works of healing and mercy which Jesus performed while on the earth, but we should fix our eyes on

His glory which was far greater than the miracles and works of wonder.

Man is more important

Consider the first: what a man is is always more important to God than what he does.

Remember that if a man had the ability to stand up and create pine trees and lakes and hills and was not a good man, through and through a good man, he would still be of no value to God!

And let us remember, too, that if a man is a good man, through and through a good man, and has no power to perform a miracle or any great work, he would still be one of God's most valued treasures. God would write his name on His own hands for it is goodness that God is looking for.

So, it was the very person and character of Jesus that was glorious. It was not only what He did—but what He was. What He did was secondary. What He was in His person was primary.

Brethren, there can be no argument about Jesus Christ's glory—His glory lay in the fact that He was perfect love in a loveless world; that He was perfect purity in an impure world; that He was perfect meekness in a harsh and quarrelsome world.

There is no end to His glory. He was perfect humility in a world where every man was seeking his own benefit. He was boundless and fathomless mercy in a hard and cruel world. He was completely selfless goodness in a world full of selfishness.

John says, "And we beheld his glory" (John 1:14). He included the deathless devotion of Jesus; the patient suffering and the unquenchable life and the grace and truth which were in the eternal Word.

I cannot help but think of this during the Christmas season of festive and generally profit-inspired celebrations. As little as it knows about the reasons for Christ coming to earth, the poor blind world is not celebrating the turning of water into wine. The celebration is not for the healing of the sick nor for the raising of the dead. The poor, blind world with what little bit of religious instinct it has really joins in celebrating what He was. Very little is said about what He did but much is said about who He was.

Everyone joins gladly in singing the songs and we all read the editorials and articles about the amazing fact that it was God walking among men; that here was a man acting like God in the midst of sinful men. This is the glory and the wonder of it all.

This is the divine glory that earth's most famous and capable personalities can never attain. This is the glory that Alexander could never reach.

Think of Alexander for a moment. That wild boy, son of Philip, trampled the civilized world under his feet, conquering everything, and then wept because there were no more worlds to conquer. But Alexander had never conquered himself and history records that he died a disappointed profligate. He was a genius in battle but a spoiled baby in his own house.

The brightness

In contrast, the glory of Jesus Christ shines like the brightness of the sun—for what He was has astonished the world. What He did was wonderful; what He said and taught was amazing; but what He was, the eternal Word made flesh, was the crown upon all that He did and all that He said.

The Bible teaches so clearly and so consistently what John proclaims in the first chapter of His Gospel: "And of his fulness have all we received, and grace for grace" (John 1:16).

Out of His fullness we have received. There is no way that it can mean that any of us have received all of His fullness. It means that Jesus Christ, the eternal Son, is the only medium through which God dispenses His benefits to His creation.

Because Jesus Christ is the eternal Son, because He is of the eternal generation and equal with the Father as pertaining to His substance, His eternity, His love, His power, His grace, His goodness, and all of the attributes of deity, He is the channel through which God dispenses all His blessing.

If you could ask the deer that goes quietly down to the edge of the lake for a refreshing drink, "Have you received of the fullness of the lake?" the answer would be: "Yes and no. I am full from the lake but I have not received from the fullness of the lake. I did not drink the lake. I only drank what I could hold of the lake."

And so, of His fullness, out of the fullness of God, He has given us grace upon grace according to our need, and it is all through Jesus Christ, our Lord. When He speaks, when He provides, while He sustains, it is because it can be said that He upholds all things by the Word of His power and in Him all things consist.

Now, here is a thought I had one day: it could have been very easy for God to have loved us and never told us. God could have been merciful toward us and never revealed it. We know that among humans it is possible for us to feel deeply and still tell no one. It is possible to have fine intentions and never make them known to anyone.

The Scriptures say that "no man hath seen God at any time, the only begotten Son, which is in the bosom of the Father, he hath declared him" (John 1:18).

The eternal Son came to tell us what the silence never told us.

He came to tell us what not even Moses could tell us.

He came to tell us and to show us that God loves us and that He constantly cares for us.

He came to tell us that God has a gracious plan and that He is carrying out that plan.

Before it is all finished and consummated, there will be a multitude that no man can number, redeemed, out of every tongue and tribe and nation.

That is what He has told us about the Father God. He has set Him forth. He has revealed Him—His being, His love, His mercy, His grace, His redemptive intention, His saving intention.

He has declared it all. He has given us grace upon grace. Now we have only to turn and believe and accept and take and follow. All is ours if we will receive because *the Word was made flesh, and dwelt among us!*

The Self-Existent God

In the beginning was the Word . . . (John 1:1)

A ny man or woman really sensitive to divine Truth discovers there is truly a kind of spiritual suffocation often felt in the attempt to wrestle with the opening verses of the Gospel of John, or with the opening verses of Genesis, for that matter.

No man is really big enough and adequate in his own faith and experience to try to expound for others these key Bible passages. No man really ought to preach on the phrase *In the beginning . . .* , but the phrase is here and in our teaching as well.

We do our best to study and learn, and there is surely a deep and helpful message for us here, but we will still sense the feeling, expressed years ago by the poet, that "fools rush in where angels fear to tread."

We must meditate on the eternal nature of God in order to worship as we should. You know I often refer to Frederick William Faber, whose great adoring heart pressed into these mysteries during his lifetime in the nineteenth century, and he celebrated the vision of God's eternal self-existence in these warm and wondrous words:

> Father! the sweetest, dearest Name
> That men or angels know!
> Fountain of life, that had no fount
> From which itself could flow!
>
> When heaven and earth were yet unmade,
> When time was yet unknown,
> Thou in Thy bliss and majesty
> Did'st live and love alone.
>
> Thy vastness is not young or old;
> Thy life hath never grown;
> No time can measure out Thy days,
> No space can make Thy throne.

Brethren, surely this must be one of the greatest and grandest thoughts we can ever know: that it is the living and eternal God with whom we are concerned, and we acknowledge that only in God can there be causeless existence!

In this context, I confess a sadness about the shallowness of Christian thinking in our day. Many are interested in religion as a kind of toy. If we could make a judgment, it would appear that numbers of men and women go to church without any genuine desire to gear into deity. They do not come to meet God and delight in His presence. They do not come to hear from that everlasting world above!

Certainly we should be aware that everything around us has a cause behind it. You have a cause and I have a cause. Everything that we know is the effect of some cause.

If we could put ourselves into some special kind of machine that would take us back and back in time, back beyond the centuries of history, beyond the beginning of the Creation, we might arrive at that point where there was nothing and no one except God Himself!

Imagining that we could erase history and everything in the universe, we would see in God causeless existence; God—self-sufficient, uncreated, unborn, unmade—God alone, the living and eternal and self-existent God.

Compared to Him, everything around us in this world shrinks in stature and significance. It is all a little business compared to Him—little churches with little preachers; little authors and little editors; little singers and little musicians; little deacons and little officials; little educators and little statesmen; little cities and little men and little things!

Brethren, humankind is so smothered under the little grains of dust that make up the world and time and space and matter that we are prone to forget that at one point God lived and dwelt and existed and loved without support, without help, and without creation.

Such is the causeless and self-existent God!

This God with whom we deal has never had to receive anything from anybody. There is no one and no thing to whom God has ever been in debt.

Some people have the brass to think they are bailing out the living God when they drop a ten dollar bill in the church offering plate on Sunday.

I do not think I exaggerate when I say that some of us put our offering in the plate with a kind of triumphant bounce as much as to say: "There—now God will feel better!"

God does not need anything

This may hurt some of you but I am obliged to tell you that God does not need anything you have. He does not need a dime of your money. It is your own spiritual welfare at stake in such matters as these. There is a beautiful and enriching principle involved in our offering to God what we are and what we have, but none of us are giving because there is a depression in heaven.

The Bible teaching is plain: you have the right to keep what you have all to yourself—but it will rust and decay, and ultimately ruin you.

Long ago God said, "If I had need of anything, would I tell you?" If the living God had need of anything He would no longer be God.

So, that was before the beginning. We are concerned here with that which the Bible calls *before the foundation of the world.*

We are told that in the beginning *God created.* We are made to realize that God does not lean upon His own creation.

If God needed help or strength, He would not be omnipotent and He would not then be God.

If God needed advice and counsel, He would not be sovereign. If He needed wisdom, He would no longer be omniscient. If He needed support and sustenance, He could not be self-existent.

So, as far as man is concerned, there was a beginning and there was a Creation. That phrase, *In the beginning,* does not mark a birth date for God Almighty. It means the point in time as we think of it when God ceased to be alone and began to make time and space and creatures and beings.

But we are not quite ready to leave that pre-creation situation, before the foundations of the earth were laid, when God dwelt alone, the uncreated Being; the Father in love with the Son, and the Son with the Holy Ghost, and the Holy Ghost with the Father and the Son.

God is the eternal God, dwelling in a tranquility that had no beginning and that can have no ending.

Now, you may note that I have not used the expression, "the pre-creation void." Void is a good and useful word. When we do not know what else to say, we call it a void.

But before the Creation, God was there and God is not a void. He is the triune God and He is all there is. In His existence before the Creation, God was already busy; busy with eternal mercies,

His mind stirring with merciful thoughts and re-demptive plans for a mankind not yet created.

This is a very good place to read Ephesians 1:4. "According as he hath chosen us in him before the foundation of the world, that we should be holy and without blame before him in love." I am well aware that sometimes when I preach I really worry the Calvinists. I know, too, that sometimes when I preach I worry the Arminians and proba-bly this is their time to sweat.

Before the creation

Paul told the Ephesian Christians that we were chosen in Christ before the creation of the world. Someone will run me around a lilac bush and say, "How can it be that you were chosen in Him be-fore the creation of the world?"

I reply with a question: "How can you explain a time when there was no matter, no law, no mo-tion, no relation, and no space, no time, and no beings—only God?"

If you can explain that to me then I can explain to you how God chose me in Him before the cre-ation of the world. I can only say that we must take into account the foreknowledge of God, for Peter wrote to his Christian brethren and called them "Elect according to the foreknowledge of God the Father, through sanctification of the Spirit, unto obedience and sprinkling of the blood of Jesus Christ . . ." (1 Peter 1:2).

The acts of Creation in the beginning were not God's first activity. God had been busy before that, for He must have been engaged in choosing and foreordaining before the foundation of the world.

Is this Calvinism?

I wrote a little editorial squib some time ago under the title, "We Travel an Appointed Way." I pointed out that we are not orphans in the world and that we do not live and breathe by accident and that we are God's children by faith. I said that it is true that our heavenly Father goes before us and that the Shepherd goes before and leads the way.

Some dear man who was among the readers wrote to me and said: "I was brought up a Methodist. In your comments, do you mean this to be foreordination? That is what the Presbyterians believe. Just what do you mean?"

I wrote him a letter, saying, "Dear Brother: When I said we travel an appointed way I was not thinking about foreordination, predestination, eternal security, or the eternal decrees.

"I was just thinking," I told him, "about how nice it is for the steps of a good man to be ordered by the Lord; and that if a consecrated Christian will put himself in the hands of God, even the accidents will be turned into blessings. Not only that, but our God will make the devil himself work for the glorification of His saints."

It has always been the experience of the children of God that when we walk daily in the will of God, even that which looks like tragedy and loss in the end will turn out to be blessing and gain.

I did not mean to go down that deep—I was just saying that our heavenly Father leads our way and that the steps of a good man are ordered by the Lord. I am sure the Methodist brother can go to sleep tonight knowing that he does not have to turn Presbyterian to be certain that God is looking after him.

By the way, I do not know how this illustration got in there, for it was not in my notes!

Now, once again to the record of the Creation, *In the beginning.*

Matter versus materialism

It is plain that God created matter—and that is not bad! Matter is that of which any physical object is composed and from matter we have obtained our words material and materialism.

I think a lot of people in our congregations get confused when some learned brother advises us that we must all join in a fervent fight against materialism.

Everyone looks around for the enemy but there seems to be no enemy in sight. If a man does not know what materialism is how can he be expected to join the battle?

The word *materialism* has become part of modern jargon. The created things that we accept as matter are all around us: things we can touch, smell, taste, handle, see, and hear. Things that yield to the senses—they are material things and they are not bad.

Materialism in its crisis form occurs when men and women created in the image of God accept and look upon matter as the ultimate. Of material and physical things they say: "These are the only reality. Matter is the ultimate—there is nothing else!"

"We must fight materialism" does not mean that everyone should get a sword and run after a fellow named Material and cut him down.

What it does mean is that we should start believing in the fact of God's Creation and that matter is only a creature of the all-wise and ever-loving God and that the physical things that we know and enjoy are not the ultimate; they are not an end in themselves.

In the Creation account, God had to have some place to put matter so He created space. He had to make room for motion so He created time.

We think of time as something wound on a great spool in heaven and that it rolls off for men faster then it does for women. Time is not like that: time is the medium in which things change. It is not time that makes a baby grow—it is change that does it. In order for change to occur, there must be a sequence of change. We call that sequence time.

And then God made the laws that govern time and space and matter. It may be an oversimplification here but in the law He established, God was just saying to matter: "Now, stretch out and let things move around."

Then, in the record, we see that God created life. He created life so there could be a consciousness of time and space and motion and matter. Then God created spirit, in order that there might be creatures who were conscious of God Himself. Then He organized the entire universe and we call it the cosmos, and thus we have the world.

Now, I suppose Creation is a great deal more complex than I have described here, and that it took longer than it is taking me to tell about it. But it was the beginning when God created the heaven and the earth. That was the beginning of human thought. That was where matter began, with time and space. That was where created life began.

Oh, how glad I am for the plain record concerning the living, loving and creating God!

God doesn't need us

I do not think I could ever worship a God who was suddenly caught unaware of circumstances in His world around me. I do not think that I could bow my knees before a God that I had to apologize for.

I could never offer myself to a God that needed me, brethren. If He needed me, I could not respect Him, and if I could not respect Him, I could not worship Him.

I could never get down and say: "Father, I know that things are going tough for You these days. I know that modernism is making it tough for the saints and I know that communism is a serious threat to the kingdom. God, I know You really need my help, so I offer myself to You."

Some of our missionary appeals are getting close to that same error: that we should engage in missionary work because God needs us so badly.

The fact is that God is riding above this world and the clouds are the dust of His feet and if you do not follow Him, you will lose all and God will lose nothing. He will still be glorified in His saints and admired of all those who fear Him. To bring ourselves into a place where God will be eternally pleased with us should be the first responsible act of every man!

All of these considerations are based upon the character and worthiness of God. Not a man or woman anywhere should ever try to come to God as a gesture of pity because poor God needs you. Oh no, no, my brother!

God has made it plain that there is a hell, a place for people who do not want to love God and do not want to serve Him. The sadness and the tragedy of this fact is that these are human beings all dear to God because He created them in His own image. Of nothing else in the Creation is it said that it was created in *the likeness of God.*

Because fallen and perishing man is still nearer to God's likeness than any other creature upon earth, God offers him conversion, regeneration and forgiveness. It was surely because of this great potential in the human personality that the Word could become flesh and dwell among us. The only begotten Son could not take upon Him the nature of angels, but He could and did take on Him the seed of Abraham, as we are told in Hebrews 2:16.

God does not waste human personality

We are assured in many ways in the Scriptures that God the Creator does not waste human personality, but it is surely one of the stark tragedies of life that human personality can waste itself. A man by his own sin may waste himself, which is to waste that which on earth is most like God.

Sin is a disease. It is lawlessness. It is rebellion. It is transgression—but it is also a wasting of the most precious of all treasures on earth. The man who dies out of Christ is said to be lost, and hardly a word in the English tongue expresses his condition with greater accuracy. He has squandered a rare fortune and at the last he stands for a fleeting moment and looks around, a moral fool, a wastrel who has lost in one overwhelming and irrecoverable loss, his soul, his life, his peace, his total mysterious personality, his dear and everlasting all!

Oh, how can we get men and women around us to realize that God Almighty, before the beginning of the world, loved them, and thought about them, planning redemption and salvation and forgiveness?

Christian brethren, why are we not more faithful and serious in proclaiming God's great eternal concerns?

How is this world all around us ever to learn that God is all in all unless we are faithful in our witness?

In a time when everything in the world seems to be vanity, God is depending on us to proclaim that He is the great Reality, and that only He can give meaning to all other realities.

How are the great unsatisfied throngs ever to discover and know that we are made by God and for Him?

The answer to the question, "Where did I come from?" can never be better answered than by the Christian mother who says, "God made you!" The great store of knowledge throughout today's world cannot improve on this simple answer.

The leading scientists can tell you of their extensive research into the secrets of how matter operates, but the origin of matter lies in deep silence and refuses to give an answer to man's many questions.

God, the self-existent God, all-knowing and all-powerful, made the heaven and the earth and man upon the earth and He made man for Himself, and there is no other answer to the inquiry, "Why did God make me?"

It is so important for us in these troubled days to be able to stand firmly and positively in this declaration: *Thus saith the Lord!*

Our chief business is not to argue with our generation, nor is it largely to persuade or prove. With our declaration, *Thus saith the Lord,* we make God responsible for the outcome. No one knows enough and no one can know enough to go beyond this. God made us for Himself: that is the first and last thing that can be said about human existence and whatever more we add is but commentary.

Eternity in Man's Heart

In him was life; and the life was the light of men.
(John 1:4)

I know there are many people who seem to find it rather easy to believe that God is eternal—but rather difficult to believe that God has put eternity, or everlastingness, into the hearts of men and women!

I have long insisted that if we had more courage we would preach more often on the image of God in man—and by that I do not mean that unconverted man is already saved.

But I do not hesitate to say that the only reason a man can be saved is that God has put eternity in his heart.

Man is fallen—yes! Man is lost, a sinner, and needs to be born again—yes! But God made man in His own image and He keeps the longing after eternity and a desire after everlasting life there within the heart of man.

The Holy Ghost, speaking through the psalmist in Old Testament times, caused him to testify: "from everlasting to everlasting, thou art God" (Psalm 90:2).

If you will trace that word everlasting in the Hebrew language, you will find that it can mean "time out of mind," or it can mean "always," or it can mean "to the vanishing point." It can also mean "to the beginningless past."

From everlasting to everlasting, God is God!

From the beginningless past to the endless future, God is God!

That is what the Holy Ghost says about the person and the eternal nature of God.

Now, if you have one of those mousetrap minds—open and shut—you will casually remark: "It is all quite simple—that is the attribute of God called eternity. You will find it in the footnote on page 71 in So and So's Systematic Theology. Now, let's go out and have a soda."

Thus you will dismiss it and leave it, or tuck it away in your memory among the unused items in the attic of your soul.

But brother, if you will let it live and the Holy Ghost is allowed to bring His radiance to it, there can be great meaning; for we are between the everlasting vanishing point of a forgotten yesterday and the equally everlasting vanishing point of an unborn tomorrow!

His own everlastingness

We take it for granted and we are not surprised at all about the eternal nature of God but the greater wonder is that God has seen fit to put His own everlastingness within the hearts of men and women.

This is really the amazing thought set down for us in Ecclesiastes 3:11—that God has made everything beautiful in His time and He has "set the world in their heart."

The word *world* used there is exactly the same word used by the Holy Ghost when He said *everlasting*. He said the nature and person of God is everlasting and then He says that within the heart of the creature named man, and whom God made in His own image, there resides this quality of everlastingness!

One translation of this passage reads: "God hath put eternity into man's mind." That is it—with a period!

It is as though God is indeed saying that He has put time out of mind into the heart of a man; that He has put the "everlasting beginningless always" into the heart of a man. It says that God has put in the heart of a man "an affinity for everlastingness."

Specialists are trying to give many reasons and explanations for the condition of mankind and I have no hesitation in speaking up about the troubled state in which men and women flounder.

I believe that this is the truth about our troubles and our problems: We are disturbed because God has put everlastingness in our hearts. He has put a longing for immortality in our beings. He has put something within men and women that demands God and heaven—and yet we are too blind and sinful to find Him or even to look for Him!

In a real sense, God has spoiled man by giving him this touch of eternity in his soul. If we were of the earth only and we belonged to the beasts, we would never be disturbed. But man cannot agree to lie down with the beast and be no more.

What, then, is the matter with man? Why does he roam and fret and fight, and like the lion in the cage, pace back and forth and roar to the heavens before he dies?

The beasts in the fields do not have any wars. The cattle in the pastures do not have any gambling dens or whorehouses. Why is it that only man among the creatures plots and schemes to form such a device as "Murder, Incorporated"?

When we say that man lives a beastly life we are insulting the beast and lying about the man! Sin is not beastly—it is devilish and the beasts of the forest are not bothered with the devil. Only people—men and women—have a rough time with the devil and the reason is plain: God has put the appreciation of everlastingness in their hearts. He has made them in His own image. He has put an inner longing for immortality in their hearts.

Once more I repeat: our preaching and our teaching do not emphasize strongly enough that

God made man in His own image. The modernists have scared us out. The Christian church is in need of many more men with backbone and intestinal fortitude—men who are not scared and cowering all the time.

Men and women need to be told plainly, and again and again, why they are disturbed and why they are upset. They need to be told why they are lost and that if they will not repent they will certainly perish. Doctors and counselors will tell troubled men and women that their problems are psychological, but it is something deeper within the human being that troubles and upsets—it is the longing after eternity!

I wrote in an article some time ago that God made man in His own image and that sin has marred the soul of man and ruined it. Then I continued, saying that when a man lifts his heart to God and prays he is doing the most natural thing in the world because God made him originally to do that very thing.

Well, some tough-minded, critical lady in an eastern state read that and fired off a sharp complaint against me to the president of The Christian and Missionary Alliance.

In charging that I was a liberal, a modernist, a heretic and a deviant in my theology, she asked for my dismissal as editor with the comment: "Just imagine, saying that prayer is a natural thing!"

I believe that some day when we both get to heaven she is going to look for one certain little editor so that she can apologize with a red face for her ignorance down here about the ways of God with men and women.

What God intended

This is exactly the fact, ladies and gentlemen: God made you with eternity in your hearts, so that when you turn your face toward the Eternal One and ask, "God have mercy on me, a sinner," and then go on to say, "Our Father in heaven," you are finally being what God intended you to be in the first place!

But when you look down at the earth like a beast, you are not being natural—you are being sinful. When you refuse to call on God through Jesus Christ, you are not doing the natural thing—you are doing the diseased thing!

My brethren, remember that sin is to human nature what a cancer is to the human body. When a man has been delivered from a cancerous growth in his body and is able to breathe and live without pain and knows that he is free—he is doing the natural thing.

So, too, when a redeemed sinner says, "The Lord is my shepherd; I shall not want," he is doing that which goes back to the garden of Eden, to the loins of Adam; yes, farther back than that to the New Adam, Jesus Christ our Lord.

I know that for sure—and I know that I am not a liberal or modernist; neither am I a fanatic nor a heretic nor a dreamer. I am just an ordinary preacher exalting God and His Christ and I think it is no compliment to anyone who cannot see that!

Yes, God has put a longing after immortality in our hearts. That is what the spirit of man wants— and he dies of suffocation when he does not get it.

I want to illustrate that. I have read that they used to take birds down into the coal mines in order to detect the presence of dangerous gases. They probably do everything by machines and devices now, but there was a time when they would take birds in their cages and leave them in any areas where it was suspected that poisonous gases might be present.

The mine owners had determined that certain birds would react quickly to the dangerous gas. If there was a high concentration of the poisonous gas, the bird would quickly fall down and die in the bottom of his cage.

Now, plainly that was a bird created by God, a miracle in feathers, a wonder with wings, created and intended to soar over the green meadows and look into the shining sun and breathe the sweet air of the heavens. But take him down into the depths of an underground mine where there is blackdamp and pollution and he quickly dies of suffocation.

You can apply that to the soul of a man. God created man a living soul and intended him to rise and mount into the eternities and live with God. The Creator made us to look back on the everlasting vanishing point that was and then on into the eternal vanishing point that will be, feeling no age and not counting birthdays, but like God, living in God!

But sin has ruined us. We have listened to that serpent, the devil. We have gone down into the isolated, dark, poison-infested pockets of the world, and men are dying everywhere of spiritual suffocation. You see them and you recognize their condition.

Some of us spent a week in Dixon, Illinois, attending the sessions of our annual district conference. I noticed one older couple staying in the hotel there. I presume they were in their late seventies. They were well dressed and they had a big car, but aging had shriveled them up. Actually, they were mean-looking and they talked to each other as if they were both in deep pain. They both looked mean and whipped as though life had done them in. Not a trace of sunshine, no fragrance and no friendliness: just two tired, weary, frustrated old people, apparently too mean to die and too old and dried up to live. I sensed they walked waiting for the undertaker!

They were just an example—the world is full of them. Hopeless and helpless human beings: some in society, in big homes and big cars. Some are in jails, in hospitals, in asylums. They make me think again of the poor birds that God made to sing and soar but are now being smothered to death in the bowels of the earth.

That is the picture of mankind. The feverish activity is one sign of what is wrong with us. Sin has plunged us into the depths and so marked us with mortality that we have become brother to the clay. We call the worm our sister and death our brother—but God never meant it to be so!

God made man upright, saying, "Now let us make man in our own image!" And in the image of God made He him and gave him dominion!

But man has sinned—and all that he has left is an appreciation of the divine and a hidden wish that he might have the eternal.

Man has not found the answer

That is the point of his vital need and that is the craving that drives him and pulls him. But he has not found the answer. He does not have that eternal life which was with the Father and was manifested unto us. Sad indeed that man in his quest can only complain that everything he finds and tries is always counterfeit!

Now, some of you are thinking that this sermon sounds like it is developing in the minor key. But I offer no apology and I make no correction. You need never come back to hear me preach again if you think I am wrong—but take this from me: there is nothing being advertised in the catalogs, being sung about or pushed over the radio, appeals from Wall Street or Hollywood or London or Singapore or Rome, not a thing in the whole world that will not turn out to be a coiled serpent in your boot if Jesus Christ does not get into it!

You know that I preached some time ago in Dr. A.B. Simpson's old tabernacle church at Times

Square in New York City. The pastor was a learned brother with a delightful southern drawl.

After I had preached several days, we were walking together in the midst of those hurrying throngs when he turned to me and said, "Brother Tozer, I think I have figured you out."

I asked him what he had discovered.

"I believe I have found your basic spiritual philosophy," he said. "I think it boils down to this: 'Everything is wrong until Jesus sets it right!' "

I replied, "Thank you, brother. That is it. I would say you have summed it up."

I had not thought about it in that way but I think he had it right, and that is where I stand, ladies and gentlemen. Everything is wrong until Jesus sets it right.

I was also asked to preach at a conference and perhaps I was wrong to go because the emphasis there is often upon fun and jokes and quips and the musicians play everything from a handsaw to a dried-up gourd. It is all very funny and something like Hollywood, I suppose.

The pastor there has since told me that after I left them his wife said to him, "Honey, after listening to Dr. Tozer, can it be true that there isn't anything good in the world?"

Well, I know she had a Bible in her house and I would consider that foolish question number 5,821 for a preacher's wife to ask.

Certainly there is nothing good. There is none that doeth good, no not one. Everything is wrong until Jesus sets it right. We all know that there are plenty of things that are considered good on the human level—but there is nothing that is divinely good until it bears the imprint of our Lord Jesus Christ.

Marks of the curse

There are three very distinct marks of the ancient curse resting upon everything in this world. First, everything is recent. Second, everything is temporal. Third, everything is transient.

As opposed to eternity, everything that man is proud of—his automatic electrical gadgets, his high-powered automobiles, his ability to go flying through the skies—all are recent. The animal man with his busy brain says, "These are the most wonderful things in the world!"

But his inner being would cry out if he would let it. "No, no! That is not the answer. That is something that belongs to the brain and to the world—but my heart is still crying for everlastingness!"

Temporal and transient things surround us—but their curse is that they belong to us only for a brief day. The curse is that man settles down in contentment, completely satisfied with the gadgets and the services which assure him every creature comfort as long as he lives.

Brother, I remind you of that day when one of those wonderful and handsome and modern vehicles will pull up to your front door. Two gray-faced men will get out with a basket and they will lug you out—away from your radio and television and electric stoves and refrigerators and sweepers and massagers—they will lug you out and someone will prepare for your funeral.

It is not the brain, it is not our human cleverness, it is not our modern progress that is going to win. If this is our pride and our desire and our joy, it is better never to have been born.

I suppose it may be more comfortable to go to hell in a Cadillac, or to pride your animal nature on food cooked in an automatic oven, but it is hell, nevertheless, when you get there.

I know I am not wrong when I warn you that your poor heart in which God has placed appreciation for everlastingness will not accept electrical gadgets and human progress in lieu of eternal life. Something inside of you is too big for that, too awesome for that, too wonderful for that! God has set the quality of everlastingness in our hearts.

So, all around us are the marks of the temporal, the transient.

I am sure you have watched a small child viewing a colorful circus parade. The great wagons, the clowns, the elephants, the lions and the tigers, the bands, the costumes, the spangles. Each thing excites the child—the eyes pop out and there are screams of delight. But it is passing. It is temporary. It is transient. The parade goes on down to the railroad station into its train and disappears.

And so it is with everything that the world has to offer us. Some kind of a pretty trinket. Some kind of a pleasing rattle to shake. Some kind of a pacifier for the scene in which we live.

When I was small, the child's pacifier was a great thing, and I suppose it still is. In my boyhood, back in the country, the pacifier never came from a store. It was a "sugar nipple"—a little cloth affair filled with sugar and then sewed up on the end. When the baby would start to squall, they just stuck this thing in his mouth—and the little fellow would stop squalling, for he was satisfied, temporarily.

I just want to make the observation that many of the preachers in our day are adept with the old-fashioned custom of the pacifier, the sugar nipple. They think it will result in more people coming to their churches. They think it will result in bigger offerings. They think that they will be more likely to be successful.

If there has to be some kind of compromise or pacifier to be crowded out, then they can go right on past as far as I am concerned.

God Almighty never said, "Young fellow, get yourself a pocketful of sugar nipples and go out and feed them to the carnal public."

What He did say was, "Preach My Word—and I will put My words in your mouth, and do not be afraid of them because if you are afraid of them I will confound you before them! But if you will be fearless I will stand with you and I will make your neck like brass!"

Consider if you will, this little old wrinkled neck of mine, with a size 15 collar. You would think that if someone bumped my head, it would come off.

But, brother, it is like brass. God Almighty said, "I will make it like brass!"

Now, we are not stopping on that note.

Dare to believe and claim

Have you dared to believe and claim this revelation from John that Jesus Christ, The Word, was with God and was God?

Have you dared to confess that great something within you that appreciates everlastingness and will not be satisfied without it?

What is it you have always really wanted?

It is not religion. You can trace that back—it is recent. It is not philosophy. It is not civilization. These you can trace back. They are recent and temporary.

We have been betrayed by every prospect that man creates.

But when we know that we are perishing, ready to perish, God's Holy Spirit is faithful, and He whispers, "In the beginning was the Word, and the Word was with God, and the Word was God" (John 1:1).

There is eternity, and eternity was made flesh and walked among us, and whoever believes in Him shall not perish but have eternal life.

The Eternal Word, the Eternal Son came to redeem us. Do you ever think as I do of the mystery of divine love and grace—how He walked around the carpenter's shop on little, rubbery legs?

Oh, a baby is a harmless thing and captures you more quickly than a regiment of soldiers. If you had seen eternity walking around on baby, rubbery legs, tumbling and falling flat among the shavings, you would have run and picked Him up and dusted Him off, whispering "It doesn't hurt. Be a big boy!" He would have smiled, shaking away a tear, and toddled off for another tumble.

That was eternity walking in flesh. It was God Almighty come to live among us to redeem us and to save us from the recent and the temporal and the transient—and to give us eternity!

Every one of us who will receive Him has that eternal life which was with the Father and was given unto men.

How wonderful that a loving God gives us this—and yet how terrible that we refuse and reject, and have to be whipped into heaven with the thongs of hell!

Oh, God offers us true Light! The sin in our nature has ruined us but He only asks that we turn to Jesus Christ and confess: "Lord Jesus, I believe You. I believe that You are the Eternal Word and that in You I have the everlastingness that is equal to God's everlastingness—that eternal life which was with the Father!"

The Redemptive Plan

He came unto his own . . . (John 1:11)

In earlier verses in John's Gospel record, we have read in remarkably brief and simple words of the eternal past and of the eternal Son. We are told that from the beginning He was God; that He made all things, and that in Him was Light and that in Him was life.

Surely, these powerfully simple words and phrases are at the root of all theology. They are at the root of all truth.

How thrilling it is for us, then, to receive in these two words, *He came,* the confirmation of the Incarnation, God come in the flesh!

I confess that I am struck with the wonder and the significance of the limitless meaning of these two words, *He came.* Within them the whole scope of divine mercy and redeeming love is outlined.

All of the mercy God is capable of showing, all of the redeeming grace that He could pour from His heart, all of the love and pity that God is capable of feeling—all of these are at least suggested here in the message that *He came!*

Beyond that, all of the hopes and longings and aspirations, all of the dreams of immortality that lie in the human breast, all had their fulfillment in the coming to earth of Jesus, the Christ and Redeemer.

Man has always been a hopeful creature, causing Milton to write that "hope springs eternal in the human breast." Even fallen man continues to be an aspiring creature. We are reminded that while mired in the pigsty, the prodigal remembered his father's house, and within himself pondered the question of "What am I doing here?"

All of our hopes and dreams of immortality, our fond visions of a life to come, are summed up in these simple words in the Bible record: *He came!* I suppose it is the editor nature within me to note that I am impressed with the fact that these two one-syllable words occupy only seven spaces in a printed line. But what these two words tell us is more profound than all of philosophy, and I am not using the superlative carelessly in this context.

There are times when the use of the superlative is absolutely necessary and you cannot escape it. The coming of Jesus Christ into this world represents a truth more profound than all of philosophy, for all of the great thinkers of the world together could never produce anything that could even remotely approach the wonder and the profundity disclosed in the message of these words, *He came!*

These words are wiser than all learning. Understood in their high spiritual context, they are more beautiful than all art, more eloquent than all oratory, more lyric and moving than all music—because they tell us that all of mankind, sitting in darkness, has been visited by the Light of the world!

Oh, I am sure that we are all too passive about what this really means! When we sing "The Light of the world is Jesus," there should be a glow on our faces that would make the world believe that we mean it.

It meant something vast and beautiful to Milton—and he celebrated the coming of Jesus into the world with one of the most beautiful and moving expressions ever written by a man.

Milton's heart was surely bowing in the Presence as he wrote:

> This is the Month, and this the happy
>   morn
> Wherein the Son of Heav'n's eternal
>   King,
> Of wedded Maid, and Virgin Mother born,
> Our great redemption from above did
>   bring;
> For so the holy sages once did sing,
>   That he our deadly forfeit should release,

And with his Father work us a perpetual
    peace.

That glorious Form, that Light
    unsufferable,
And that far-beaming blaze of Majesty,
Wherewith he wont at Heav'n's
    high Council Table
To sit the midst of Trinal Unity,
He laid aside; and here with us to be,
    Forsook the Courts of everlasting Day,
And chose with us a darksome House
    of mortal Clay.

See how from far upon the Eastern road
The star-led Wizards haste with odors
    sweet:
Oh run! prevent them with thy humble
    ode,
And lay it lowly at his blessed feet;
Have thou the honor first thy Lord to greet,
    And join thy voice with the Angel Choir,
From out his secret Altar toucht with
    hallow'd fire.

Such was Milton's poetic description of his feel-
ings and his understanding of the Incarnation.

For myself, I am one who is just plain childishly
glad that He came!

It is the grandest story of all the ages—yet
many of us sit and listen and then we yawn and
inwardly confess, "I am bored!"

The reason?

I think we have heard it and heard it again so many times that it no longer means to us all that it should.

Oh, brethren—these wonderful and beautiful and mysterious words—*He came!*

His own

Then we read that "He came unto his own, and his own received him not" (John 1:11).

There is a significant fact in the use of these words, *his own*. In their double use in this passage in the English language, the words seem to be the same.

But, as used by John, the translation of the first is that He came unto His own things, His own world, His own home.

One translation says, "He came unto His own home."

The second use then is different—as though "the people in His own world did not receive Him."

Let us think about His world to which He came—for it is Christ's world. The world we buy and sell and kick around and take by force of arms—this world is Christ's world. He made it and He owns it all.

Jesus Christ, the eternal Word, made this world. He made the very atoms of which Mary was made; the atoms of which His own body was made. He made the straw in that manger upon which He was laid as a newborn baby.

I have given much thought to this sweetest and tenderest of all the mysteries in God's revelation to man.

I confess that I would have liked to have seen the baby Jesus. That is not a possibility—for death has no more dominion over Him, and He is glorified yonder at the right hand of the Majesty on high. But that same Jesus, now ascended and glorified, was that baby Jesus once cradled in the manger straw. Taking a body of humiliation, He was still the Creator who made the wood of the manger, made the straw and was Creator of all the beasts that were there. In truth, He had made the little town and all that it was. He had also made the star that lingered over the scene that night.

This was the eternal One. He had come into His own world. While we often talk about Him being our guest here, it is not Jesus Christ who is the guest.

We talk about making God partner in our affairs but I dare to tell people that they should stop patronizing Jesus Christ. He is not the guest here—He is the host!

We are the guests and we are here by sufferance. It is time for us to stop apologizing for the Lord Jesus Christ and start apologizing for ourselves!

We have a lot of apologists who write books and give lectures apologizing for the person of Christ and trying to "explain" to our generation that the Bible does not mean "exactly" what it says.

God has revealed Himself in Jesus Christ and thus we know where we stand, believing that "through him all things were made; and without him nothing was made that has been made."

Jesus Christ made the world in which we live and He placed all of the stars and planets in their courses throughout the universe.

Can any man believe that God really needs him and commissions him to run around apologizing and explaining, rushing in to take God's part and setting up a logical defense for the eternal, omniscient and omnipotent God?

The earthly relationship

I am going to digress here to make a further point concerning the earthly relationship of this eternal One who came unto His own world.

I hear an occasional devotional exercise on the radio in which the participants ask: "Mary, mother of God, pray for us."

Mary is dead and she is not the mother of God. It is only right that we should express our position based on the Word of God.

If Mary is the mother of God, then Elizabeth is God's cousin. You can check back and if that is true, then God has a wide assortment of cousins and uncles and grandchildren—all to the point of absurdity.

Mary is not the mother of God, for the Holy Ghost said in the Scriptures, "A body hast thou prepared me" (see Hebrews 10:5; Psalm 22:9–10; Philippians 2:7–8).

Mary was the mother of that tiny babe. God in His loving and wise plan of redemption used the body of the virgin Mary as the matrix to form a body for His eternal Son, who was with the Father and was Himself God.

For love and faith and humility we honor Mary. She was chosen of God to be the recipient of the eternal Son and to give that Son a human body.

That is why we do not join in saying, "Mary, mother of God." We should always refer to her as "Mary, mother of Christ." Then we have it right and we have given Mary her proper honor, for it is an honor higher than given to any other woman since time began.

I have expressed this here because Jesus Christ, the eternal Word, made this world. He knew what He was doing when He made us in the image of God and He does not want us to compromise or rationalize on His behalf.

What does He want from us? The way in which we can most perfectly please Him is to render to Him the total commitment of our beings! Every one of us needs to bow and kneel before Him, confessing that we are sinners, with the earnest prayer: "Oh, Lord, touch me and make me whole!"

Then we are able to stand on our feet, cleansed and forgiven, no longer crawling in the mire and degradation of the darkness. It is then that we can stand up and looking to the heavens, sing with feeling and assurance:

I was once a sinner, but I came
Pardon to receive from my Lord,
This was freely given, and I found
That He always keeps His word.

In the Book 'tis written, Saved by grace;
Oh, the joy that came to my soul!
Now I am forgiven and I know
By the blood I am made whole!

We belong to God. We belong to His Christ. This is our Father's world. Everything we touch and handle belongs to Him. The breezes that blow, the clouds above, the fields of corn and waving wheat, the tall, noble forests and the flowing rivers—they are all His!

We have come to love Him and adore Him and honor Him—but we do not patronize and we do not apologize.

Yes, He came in the fullness of time, and His own world, the world of nature, received Him. But His own people received Him not!

It is my own feeling that when Jesus came, all of nature went out to greet Him. The star led the wise men from the East. The cattle in the stable stall in Bethlehem did not bother Him.

His own things in created nature received Him.

Dr. G. Campbell Morgan in his volume called *The Crisis of the Christ,* points out that when Jesus went into the wilderness to be tempted of the devil, He was there with the wild beasts for forty days and nights.

Dr. Morgan believed that there had been a wrong conception about Jesus being with the animals, as though they had been wanting to attack Him and that He had to have angelic protection.

Dr. Morgan said, properly, "That is not true. The wild beasts recognized their King, and no doubt they crept to His feet and licked them."

In harmony with the natural world

Jesus was perfectly safe there—He was nature's Creator and Lord. He was in harmony with nature. As He grew in stature and wisdom, I think the wind blew for His pleasure and the very earth on which He trod smiled. The stars at night looked down on the cottage of that Man known as the humble carpenter.

Let me venture an opinion here. Jesus was in harmony with nature in this world and I am of the opinion that the deeper our own Christian commitment becomes the more likely we will find ourselves in tune and in harmony with the natural world around us.

Some people have always scoffed at the habits of St. Francis as though he probably was not in his right mind. I have come to believe that he was so completely yielded to God, so completely and fully taken up with the Presence of the Holy Ghost that all of nature was friendly to him.

He preached to the birds, he called the rain and the wind his friends and the moon his sister. His life contained many and unusual delights because God's blessed world received him so fully and so warmly.

Brethren, I am not ashamed of his world—I am only ashamed of man's sin. If you could take all of the sin out of this world, suddenly extract it, there would be nothing in all the world to be ashamed of and nothing to be afraid of.

Take away the sin and there would be no more sickness and disease. There would be no patients in the mental asylums. Crime would be a thing of the past and you could go to bed at night and leave all the doors unlocked.

That is why I have repeated we have no business making excuses for God. Our apologies must be for humanity—and for our sins.

I believe that Jesus carried a perfect body to Calvary but there, dying on the cross, all of our human filth, our sins and sicknesses and diseases, were all laid on Him.

He had come into His own world, where even the winds and waves obeyed His least command. We call those events miracles, but really it was just God Almighty acting like God in the world that received Him.

But when we come to consider the people, proud humanity with all of its sin and sicknesses and death—that is another story!

In the fullness of time, it was the nation of Israel, the Jews, to whom Jesus came. Of all the people on the earth, the nation of Israel surely was the best prepared to receive Him because they were the children of Abraham, called to be a chosen people in an everlasting covenant with God the Father.

Israel had the revelation of God. The Israelites knew all the traditions of worship and faith. They had the prophets. They had the temple worship and the observances of the holy days.

Yet having all of these, they failed to recognize Jesus as Messiah and Lord. There is no doubt that theirs was the greatest moral blunder in the history of mankind, for He came to His own people and His own people rejected Him! Oh, the blindness of it all when the Jews turned Him away.

The Bible is very plain in warning us and telling us of that kind of spiritual blindness.

In earlier and troubled times in the nation, God had commissioned Isaiah as His prophet, telling him: "Go, and tell this people, Hear ye indeed, but understand not; and see ye indeed, but perceive not. Make the heart of this people fat, and make their ears heavy, and shut their eyes; lest they see with their eyes, and hear with their ears, and understand with their heart, and convert, and be healed" (Isaiah 6:9-10).

This was the kind of blindness that lay upon them when He came and they did not recognize Him. It was a stroke of God Almighty upon them for sin. They rejected Him.

His own people received Him not—and the question follows, "Why?"

First of all, I think it would have meant probable financial loss for many to step out of their situations in life and follow Jesus. The rich young ruler who came to Jesus to ask questions is a good example of that position. He was interested in the teachings of Jesus and asked what he should do. Jesus gave him a test of discipleship, urging him to dispose of his properties and join the disciples in following Him. But the young man made his choice and went away sorrowing, for he had great possessions.

I am afraid that humanity's choice would still be the same today—people are more in love with their money and their possessions than they are with God.

Second, for many of those men and women who considered the claims of Christ in His day, following Jesus would have called for abrupt and drastic changes in their pattern of living. They could not tolerate the thought of allowing the selfish and proud aspects of their lives to be disturbed.

I think a third factor was their almost complete disdain for the inward spiritual life which Jesus taught as a necessity for mankind. When Jesus insisted that it is the pure in heart who will see God, that it is the humble mourner who will be comforted and that the meek will inherit the earth—all of this meant a great housecleaning inwardly.

In our day history repeats itself—many who want to follow the Christian traditions still balk and reject a thoroughgoing spiritual housecleaning within their beings.

Fourth, Jesus brought forth a whole new concept among humans that the first shall be last in the kingdom—and that the person who will be a committed Christian must know the meaning of complete abdication of self.

The centuries have not changed this. Jesus still calls with a definite challenge that "Then said Jesus unto his disciples, If any man will come after me, let him deny himself, and take up his cross, and follow me" (Matthew 16:24).

Fifth, Jesus talked about the necessity of the genuineness of faith—faith in the unseen; faith that has no dependence upon the works of the Law; faith that does not stake its trust on the temple or the traditions.

Jesus taught frankly that He was asking His followers to throw themselves out on God. For the multitudes, He was asking too much. He had come from God—but they received Him not!

Now, coming back to the responsibilities of men and women in our own day—it seems to be a very satisfying thing for some to just sit back and belabor the Jews. It is very comforting for us, two thousand years removed, to preach about the Jews who did not receive Him. It is a kind of safety valve for us, a red herring that we draw across the trail, as though it will take God's eyes away from our own sins and our own rejections.

Jesus taught very plainly that we should take the beam from our own eyes in order to see clearly to remove the mote from our brother's eye.

Every one of us should be warned about this kind of self-deception in matters of spiritual responsibility. We have two thousand years of

Christian teaching and preaching that the Jews did not have. We have a revelation that the Jews did not have, for we have both the Old and the New Testaments. We have information and spiritual light that the Jews did not have in their time.

Then, too, we have an urgency by the presence of the Holy Spirit which the Jews did not have.

In short, I do not think for one minute that we ought to spend our time belaboring the Jews and comforting our own carnal hearts by any emphasis that Israel rejected Him. If we do, we only rebuild the sepulchers of our fathers, as Jesus said.

Brethren, history tells us that they did what they wanted to do. They knew their spiritual responsibilities but they still rejected Jesus when He came into their midst.

The same situation is all around us today. Millions of men and women with an understanding of the revelation of God in Jesus Christ, with many years of spiritual light and Bible teaching in their backgrounds, still are not willing to receive and commit themselves to Him whom the very angels and stars and rivers receive. They hesitate and they delay because they know God is asking the abdication of their own selfish little kingdom and interest.

Some go "underground"

I know that some of you are not going to change your way of living. You will go "underground" before you will do that. As far as some people are concerned, I am sure that all of my preaching has only the result of driving them underground. They will not consent to the thorough inward housecleaning that is involved in full commitment to Christ.

Forgiveness and cleansing and purity! I will tell you this about the manger stall in which they laid the baby Jesus—it was clean. It was simple, it was plain—even rude by our standards, but I know it was clean. Joseph and Mary would never have let the baby Jesus lie there in a dirty crib—and it is just as true today that our Lord will not inhabit any place that is not clean.

Some people would rather have the dirt than to have the presence of the Son of God. They prefer to stay in the darkness than to come to the Light of the world. They have every opportunity to come. They have every kind of spiritual light. But they will not receive Him—they do not want their spiritual houses to be clean.

This is the tragedy of mankind, my brethren. We have rejected Him from our hearts because we must have our own way. The true meaning of Christianity is a mystery until we have been converted and brought in by the miracle-working, transforming power of the new birth. Until Jesus Christ is sincerely received, there can be no knowledge of salvation, nor any understanding of the things of God.

The little, selfish, sinful man rejects the Son of God. While he is still enumerating the things he desires and the things he wants, the Son of God stands outside.

"He came . . . and his own received him not" (John 1:11).

My brethren, I repeat: that is the great tragedy of mankind!

Divine Love Incarnate

For God so loved the world, that he gave his only begotten Son, that whosoever believeth in him should not perish, but have everlasting life. (John 3:16)

If we were to judge John 3:16 on the basis of its value to the human race, we would have to say that it is probably the most precious cluster of words ever assembled by the mind of an intelligent man; a twenty-five-word compendium in which is contained the eternal Christian evangel, the message of genuine good news!

When we begin to grasp the radiance and significance of this text, we sense that it is as though God has compressed all of the deepest and richest meaning of the Scriptures into one brief, glorious segment of truth.

We learn in school that diamonds are made from native carbon which has been placed under tremendous pressure which in time brings about the process of crystallization.

If we will just let our imaginations soar a bit, we can properly say that the Holy Ghost has taken the redemptive evangel and has placed it under the emotional pressure of the triune God, so unbelievably strong and powerful that it has been crystallized into this shining diamond of truth.

Using our imaginations again, I believe that if we could place this John 3:16 text on one side of some vast eternal scale held in space by some holy one to measure its value to mankind, it would prove to be more precious than all of the books that have ever been written by men.

There have been unusual men of great intellect and learning and understanding in the history of mankind. We immediately think back to Plato and Aristotle and that cluster of great minds several hundred years before the coming of Jesus into the world. Yet I would seriously say and would contend that if everything all of them had written could be placed in one side of a measure and John 3:16 in the other, they would all prove to be as light as air by comparison.

I have had a lifetime of reading and thinking and praying—yes, and trusting, too, but I am willing to say seriously that if we could test the true value of all the works of Shakespeare, the sonorous compositions of Milton, and everything produced by Scott and Victor Hugo and Emerson

and Bacon, and all the rest—all of them put together could not compare in value to what these
twenty-five words mean to the human race.

That is how highly I value the declaration of
John 3:16.

I have heard that John 3:16 is a favorite preaching
text for young preachers, but I confess that as far as I
can recall, I have never had the courage to prepare
and preach a sermon with John 3:16 as my text. I
suppose I have quoted it as many as 15,000 or 20,000
times in prayer and in testimony, in writing and in
preaching, but never as a sermon text.

One of the noble old commentators of the nineteenth century, Allicott, said something like this
when he came to John 3:16 in his textual comments: "I do not intend to say very much about
this text. It is a favorite of younger preachers, but
old men feel it is better felt than talked about."

Profound appreciation

I think my own hesitation to preach from John
3:16 comes down to this: I appreciate it so pro-
foundly that I am frightened by it—I am overwhelmed by John 3:16 to the point of inadequacy,
almost of despair. Along with this is my knowledge that if a minister is to try to preach John 3:16
he must be endowed with great sympathy and a
genuine love for God and man.

However, this time I am engaged in a continu-
ing series in the Gospel of John and this burning
bush is before us in the way. I cannot go around it
and I dare not flee from it!

So, I approach it. I approach it as one who is filled with great fear and yet great fascination. I take off my shoes, my heart shoes, at least, as I come to this declaration that *God so loved the world.*

This is more than a thought—it is a divine message, worthy of enunciation by an archangel. It can be restated and that is all that I can hope to do with it.

I can restate it in a more personal application, for it has this significance to me: it tells me that I mean something to God. It tells me that I am precious to Him. God wants to reveal Himself to us in personal terms. He wants to show us that in loving the world He loves each one of us individually because we mean something to Him. We matter to Him. God himself is emotionally concerned about each of us.

If I told you only those three things about God and His love and you have been listening with your heart as well as your ears, I could send you off with a benediction knowing it would have been well worth your trip, no matter how far you had come.

The fact that God so loved the world, restated in personal terms, means that God is emotionally concerned about you!

It means that you matter to God. It is a statement that you mean something to God.

This brings us to a strange contradiction in human nature: the fact that a person can reek with pride, display a swollen ego and strut like a peacock—and still be the loneliest and most miserable person in the world.

These people are all around us, pretending and playing a game. Deep within their beings they are almost overwhelmed by their great loneliness, by that heavy sense of being actually an orphan in the final scheme of things.

Such an individual is well aware that he is alone in spite of being busy and active—for in the things that matter, he is an orphan. In the sense in which we speak, he has no father to whom he can run. There is no mother to whom he can go for comfort.

His inward feeling tells him that there is no one anywhere who is emotionally concerned about him.

Any concern of his own narrow little family is not the answer to his need for they will all die along with him.

The result of this strange, aching sense of loneliness and cosmic orphanage for a human being may be summed up like this:

"What good is it to be a human being? No one cares about me.

"I matter to no one except the little mortal circle around me and when they go, I will matter to no one!"

This complex is one of the bitter results of sin, for the same devil that once came and said to Eve, *Did God really say . . . ?* was saying, in effect: "You don't really matter to God. God has lied to you!"

We have to say that Eve believed Satan's lie, the lie that God was not concerned about her and that God had no emotional connection with her life and being. Thus sin came into the world with all of its woes and its ugly trail of death along with it.

God made us as we are

The truth is that God has made us as we are: so vast, so complex and with such tremendous intellectual and spiritual capacities. It is only sin and defeat and death that can bring us to this sense of orphanage, this sense of having been put out of our father's house and the feeling that follows when the house is burned down and the father is dead.

This is where the unregenerated person is in today's world. This is why the Napoleons and the Hitlers and the Stalins rise up in their efforts to conquer and prevail and immortalize themselves. They try to arrange it so that when they are gone the world will remember, and they mistakenly think that someone will care!

This explains, also, the story of the poet who looked back on his life after many years, remembering that as a small boy, he "wrote on high a name I deemed would never die."

But when he went back to the scene of his boyhood when he was eighty and saw his name carved there in crude, boyish lettering, he smiled—but he was ashamed. He was a human being and he recalled that craving in his once-youthful life, the craving to matter to someone, to mean something to someone.

Now, there is something in this context that we must seriously consider, for the hour in which we live happens to be the hour of a great humanistic tide.

In this humanistic approach, the individual is no longer the concern. The individual really does not matter anymore in the kind of society in which we live.

We are pressed to think of the human race in a lump.

We are schooled to think of the human race in terms of statistics.

We are taught to think of the human race as we might think of a breed of hens; the populace, all related intrinsically, but the individual does not count.

This is the curse of statism. That is the curse of dictatorship philosophy and the weapon of the totalitarian governments back to the days of the old Roman Empire and down through the more modern Nazi and Fascist and Communist ideologies.

The state is made to be everything. The party or the organization means everything but the individual means nothing at all.

God deals with individuals

Into the very face and strength of this kind of humanism in our day comes the Christian evangel, wondrously alight, with the assurance for everyone who will listen:

"You are an individual and you matter to God. His concern is not for genus and species but with the individuals He has created."

When the eternal Son of God became the Son of Man and walked on the earth, He always called individuals to His side.

He did not preach to the multitudes as though they were a faceless crowd. He preached to them as individuals and with a knowledge of the burdens and the needs of each one.

The individuals mattered to Him. He was emotionally concerned with the individual beings.

The woman whose accusers said she was taken in the act of adultery was lying in the dust ready to be stoned to death, but the Son of Man raised her gently to her feet. He assured her of God's forgiveness for the individual as He told her to go and sin no more.

It was not easy for women as individuals on this earth two thousand years ago. The gospel record is plain, however, that Jesus selected mothers from the crowds and touched and blessed their infants and assured them individually that "for of such is the kingdom of God" (Mark 10:14).

Oh, my brethren, Jesus did not come into our world to deal with statistics!

He deals with individuals and that is why the Christian message is and always has been: God loves the world.

It is not that God just loves the masses. He loves the masses and the throngs only because they are made up of individuals. He loves every individual person in the world.

Now, it seems that the world does not know that individual factor in the love of God.

I think I am beginning to understand what Dwight Moody said at one time about the effect of God's love. He is quoted as having said, "If I could get everybody in the world to believe God loves them, I would get everybody in the world converted!"

That may have been an overstatement but at least I think I agree with him that too many individuals think of God's love just being for the world in a lump—and the individual is not involved.

You have only to look around you with a serious kind of observation to confirm the fact that the devil has been successful in planting his lie that no one cares about the individual person.

Even in nature around us, there appears to be very little individualistic concern. The burden of concern is always for the species.

The poet Tennyson said of nature: "So careful of the type she seems; so careless of the single light."

Nature has planted within every normal human being the tremendous urge for self-propagation and that urge guarantees the perpetuation of the race.

Yet, when the individual has perpetuated his kind he dies and goes back to the dust. All of the tribes that walk the earth today are but a handful compared to those that slumber in its bosom.

Since the long flight of years began, matron and maid and soldier and kings, learned men and fools, men in the great bloom of their old age, all lie down together.

Who really cares about the past generation?

Nature seems to confirm the idea that you and I matter very little in the great scheme of the vast universe. Fallen nature seems to confirm the notion held by so many weary and dying men and women: "Few there are that care when we live and fewer still when we die."

We will eternally thank God for the Christian message and the Christian hope and the miracle of transformed human lives that assures us that God cares and that He loves us individually.

We will eternally thank God also that His care and concern are not tailored for the nice people and the respectable people and those who have some means of helping themselves.

No one stops to think very much about the old tramp who shuffles into the mission hall. Sure, he is a bum. His old clothes fit him as if he had been born in them. His old, tired body seems to smell of every place he has been in during the past 10 years.

When he is sober enough, he still has those thoughts and memories of his boyhood and of those who loved him and nurtured him. Now he is only told to "Move on, buddy"; turned away even from the places where tramps find some refuge.

He feels only the solitude of a vast and gusty universe. Blown about like the grains of dust or the leaves of autumn, he knows only the deep sense of sadness and complete orphanage, as though all that had meant anything had died.

In the past and to this moment, the Christian evangel continues to confront all of the hopeless and the helpless in every culture and in every land, insisting:

"Wait a minute, you! You with the dirt and the whiskers and smell and hollow sunken cheeks, wait a minute.

"Some One is emotionally concerned about you!

"Some One who matters is not happy because you are the way you are. He is One who knows your name. He remembers you and loves you where you are and as you are. You mean something to Him!"

Then some smiling person, happy and blest in the grace and mercy of the caring Savior, whispers to that needy one, "God so loved you that He gave His only begotten Son that whosoever—and that includes you—whosoever believeth in Him should not perish, but have everlasting life!"

He knows very well that he does not matter to the mayor of the city. He knows that he does not matter to the chief of police. He knows that he is not in the heart of the governor or the president or the members of the president's cabinet.

But the shining beauty and the radiance of the message finally get through to him:

"You matter to the living and loving God of all creation. Above everyone else in the whole universe, He cares for you and calls to you and has gracious plans for you!"

The diamond of truth

That is the high compression. That is the dazzling facet of the diamond of truth which God has thrown almost with a happy carelessness out to the world, saying, "Take it!"

What a message for the sinner! What a message for the failure. What a message for the loneliest of the lonely. What a message for men and women who have drifted far from God after learning the important Bible verses in a godly home and in Sunday school!

What about the boys who have gone to the wars? What about the helpless men and women in hospitals and institutions? What about those who find themselves lying in the wreckage and debris of some tragic accident? What about those who have come to their senses but are still bound by chains of habits and abuse and self-gratification?

How many have turned their eyes upward to the God above and said, "Oh God, when I was a child they often told me that I mattered to You. Is it any different now? Have You changed Your mind, God?"

The records are not all in yet, but in many places and in many instances, the ancient but gracious voice of God has stirred into memory the promises of God to those who will believe and trust:

"No, child, nothing with God has changed. The promises are still available. Grace and mercy are still flowing. I am not happy about your condition for I love you so that I have given my one and only Son that whoever believes in Him shall not perish, but have eternal life."

Now, I am going to say something here that I do not establish as anyone's official doctrine, but I am quite certain that there are Christian mothers who grieve over boys who they feel are in hell today.

Some of those children will greet us in that happy day of everlasting reunion.

Do you not think that the thief on the cross had a mother?

And do you not think the thief on the cross was in the tender heart of his mother as he faced death?

Do you not suppose that the mother thought within herself: "I have failed him and society has failed him and he has failed society. He is dying the death of a criminal. My boy, my boy!"

What that mother did not know was that the One who loves and cares was within touching distance. What she did not know was that the young rebel and traitor turned his eyes to the One who cared and with faith said, "Remember me when thou comest into thy kingdom" (Luke 23:42).

Our dying Lord Jesus answered him with the reassurance: "Verily I say unto thee, Today shalt thou be with me in paradise" (23:43).

The mother only knew that her boy had died by execution, and her hair was grayer and her face more tired and her gloom heavier when that day was over and she knew he was dead.

What she did not know was that someone else in the universe loved and cared and forgave to an extent far beyond a mother's love. She did not know that an eternal One who had come to save His people from their sins was emotionally involved—her son mattered in God's sight.

Men had taken her son from a cell. They had taken him to the execution. But now he matters. Suddenly he becomes significant in his confession of faith and there is not an angel in the winged choir above more significant than he. His name as one of the redeemed sounds yonder in God's promised heaven because the Christian message says, *God so loved!*

Thankfully, brethren, that love is not the love for a species but a love for individuals.

We are right when we sing the words, "Jesus, lover of my soul." We are wrong if we sing, "Jesus, lover of the human race."

In the strictest sense, there is no human race. The race is composed of individuals and if you take away the individuals you have no human race.

There is such a thing as a crowd and sometimes evangelists love to preach to a crowd. But the crowd is simply a congregation of individuals.

Each individual has eternal significance

In the light of His love, let us always remember that every individual has eternal significance and meaning in the heart of God and that He is emotionally concerned with the individual.

This is still God's day of grace and mercy and willingness to forgive, and there is not a human being anywhere who has been written off and cast out as being "no good and absolutely hopeless."

God says plainly that there is none righteous and that we must be saved and that we will perish if we do not repent. But in the sense of being hopeless and beyond forgiveness and impossible of conversion—there is not one.

I advise you not to listen to any would-be interpreters of truth who insist that God has chosen some to be saved and has given up on the rest and that those He has not chosen are no good, vessels of wrath fitted to destruction and created by God for the fun of damning them.

Do not listen to those who teach what Wesley called "a horrible decree."

I have never said that there is good in everybody, but I say there is Someone who loves and cares for them whether they are good or not. I say that there is a loving God who is emotionally concerned about them.

We often go away from church talking carelessly about a lot of things, but I want you to be saying to one another: "The One who was with the Father and who came down and reported what He saw, says plainly that we matter to God as individuals; and that He came down from above not to condemn the world but that the world might be saved and live."

I have counseled people who have said to me, "Dr. Tozer, I want to believe what God says but I have sinned, I have lied, I have failed. I have made vows and broken them. I have made promises and failed to keep them. I am just no good!"

And amazing, also, that all of that recrimination takes place after God himself has gone to the trouble of proclaiming His love and assuring us that we do matter to Him.

God has never indicated that He is waiting for us to make ourselves morally good. He has indicated, however, that we have a potential that He well knows and He is waiting to make us over to bring glory to Him and to prove the wisdom of His mercy and grace throughout eternity.

Now, I can only point out that faith cometh by hearing the Word and that it begins to work as soon as we begin to affirm it.

Our part is to turn to God in faith, confessing our great need, and thanking Him for revealing His love and concern for us through Jesus Christ, the eternal Son.

Faith cometh by hearing and faith becomes perfect as you pray and talk with God, your heavenly Father. He longs to hear you confide in Him: "Oh God, I do believe I matter to you and I do believe in Jesus Christ as my Savior and Lord."

Perhaps this sounds too simple: frankly, it is simple and easy to come into the arms of God by faith!

Come to Him for the first time as a sinner, for forgiveness and salvation.

Come back to God if you have wandered away. Come back home if you have strayed.

Every one of us must come with full confidence that it is a personal word God has spoken to us in this greatest of all proclamations, that "God so loved the world that he gave his only begotten Son, that whosoever believeth in him should not perish, but have everlasting life."

The Divine Intention

For God sent not his Son into the world to condemn the world; but that the world through him might be saved. (John 3:17)

The compelling message of John 3:17 is more than a statement of God's intention towards the human race, for in actuality it constitutes a "proclamation extraordinary!"

It is a three-part proclamation joined beautifully to John 3:16. We are thus assured that God sent His Son into the world; that He did not send Him to condemn the world; and that He sent Him in order that the world might be saved.

Because I have been so involved with this passage in my preparation, waking up to it, walking with it, meditating over it, I have a burning question within me that I must ask. I suspect that it might be called "the unanswered question."

It is not a question about any interpretation of this portion of John's Gospel.

It is rather a question about our human reactions to such a moving proclamation from the living God:

Why is there a blank kind of indifference and why is there an incredible apathy to such an extraordinary proclamation of God's best intentions for us?

It is not a sufficient answer to say that unregenerated people are indifferent to spiritual things. It needs to be said plainly that there is also an amazing apathy and dullness even among professing Christians in our churches.

This is a gravely significant message from the heart of God Himself, yet even in the full light of it, people are indifferent.

Upon our eyes there seems to have fallen a strange dimness.

Within our ears there seems to have fallen a strange dullness.

In our minds there is a stupor, and in our hearts, I am afraid, there is a great callousness.

It is a wonder, and a terrible responsibility, that we should have this message from the heart of God in our possession and be so little stirred up about it!

Now, if we had never had this communication from God, I could possibly understand why we could go on our way and as Tennyson said, "nourish a dumb life within the brain like sheep."

If we had no personal word from the Lord, then I could see why we could all come to church and sit in stoical silence; why we could kneel in prayer and mumble into a deaf ear that does not hear; why we could rise in the morning and be more concerned about whether the newspaper has arrived than about spiritual and eternal verities.

If this verse had never been entrusted to us, I might be able to explain our indifference and apathy.

I could say, "It is the indifference of despair, or the apathy of despair." I could use the illustration of the Israelites in the bondage of despair in Egypt, as generation followed generation in slavery. They had no hope of ever having it otherwise. They had no expectation.

If this verse were not here I would know why we are the way we are. If this proclamation extraordinary had not been made, I might understand how we can be so unhappy. I might understand how humans can walk around looking down at the earth like the beasts and rarely looking at the sky.

But in the light of the fact that it was made known 2,000 years ago, I can only ask: What is the matter with us? Why is there so little response? Why does this great stupor lie upon us as it does?

Some think that we are spiritual people and that we belong to spiritual churches. In all frankness, I think many would change their minds if they knew how little response there is, how little sensitivity to the Spirit, how little urgency of the heart in spiritual matters.

A victory for evil

I do believe that this apathy that is upon us is a tactical victory for organized evil. And I am not referring to organized crime. I do not know too much about the dark spirits that move up and down in the world and I want to know even less as I grow nearer to God in grace!

But I know the Bible teaches that there are sinister spirits walking up and down. The Bible speaks of them as principalities and powers and dominions. They are undoubtedly abroad, invisible to the naked eye, inaudible to the ear, but they are the legions of hell. They are the fifth column of iniquity, present in the world, and their business is to subvert and traduce and destroy and bind and kill, like the thief that gets into the fold.

Their business is to beat the propaganda of hell into human minds until we are groggy and punch drunk and without lift in aspiration or hope and without immortal dreams. I believe that is the tactical victory for the devil all around us.

Then, too, I believe that the very dull and gloomy countenances that Christians wear are an astonishment to the unfallen creatures yonder.

The Bible speaks of the unfallen beings, the watchers, the holy ones, angels and archangels. They are holy creatures who have continued faithfully in serving and worshiping the living God.

I do not know how much they know—but they must know something!

They were sent to joyfully announce the birth of Jesus in the fullness of time.

They were later sent to announce the Resurrection of Jesus.

In the book of Revelation we are told of their flight in midheaven and of their movements among men. So they must be here.

I repeat, then, that the manner in which we can take God's love and concern with such indifference must be an astonishment to holy creatures.

Christians offer many excuses for their lack of interest and enthusiasm about the things which matter most to the heart of God.

Some excuse themselves on the basis of comparison with others whom they call extremists and fanatics.

"We are more sober in personality. We are better educated. We are more cultured and that is why we display so little of our emotions!"

If I thought such an answer to be the truth, I would say, "Thank God." But I do not think it is the truth at all.

In our own fellowship, as soon as the benediction is pronounced, anyone would be hard pressed to hear the archangel Gabriel if he tried to blow his horn just a few feet over our heads. Suddenly we are in high gear with our talk and noise and human exuberance with one another.

Brethren, the fact that we can deal with God's love and mercy and grace with an almost complete silence and indifference is not a proof of our own culture, but a proof of our sin! It is not a proof that we are well educated, but proof that we are afflicted with hardness of heart!

Our attitudes about God and His love can result in a victory for organized evil and may well be an astonishment to unfallen creatures, but that is not all.

A great grief

I believe that our attitudes must be a great grief to God Himself, as He tries to move us to praise and delight and devotion.

I surely believe that it is the nature of God to delight in enthusiasm and I do not refer to the extreme aspects of fanaticism.

I refer back to the record concerning the warmth and brightness and enjoyment of our Lord when He walked with us on this earth. I read and study and am assured that the Lord Jesus Christ had a special fondness for the babies and the small children and I think I know why.

These little ones are always vigorous and buoyant and unsophisticated and fresh. Their reactions are unmediated, candid, and truthful. They do just what they do out of simplicity showing the immediate response of their young hearts.

Jesus called the children and laid His hands upon them and blessed them, and then taught that "for of such is the kingdom of God" (Mark 10:14).

As a result, the theologians have been tossing that statement around ever since wanting to know what it all means!

The simple-hearted people knew that Jesus just loved the babies because they were innocent and honest and unspoiled. They responded to Him and to His love without stopping to consider and measure all of the consequences.

A small child is never concerned with putting on a front as adults so often do when they would like to have others believe that they are something more than they really are.

In his famous work on human conceit, Wordsworth pictures us when we are born as coming down from the hand of God trailing clouds of glory. He shows a little bit of heaven trailing around the growing boy.

Then, as the lad travels farther and farther from home, sad and tragic as it may be, the glory evaporates away and finally disappears. That little bit of heaven that once surrounded the newborn boy disappears like dew before the sun, until there is no longer any glory remaining.

The lad becomes the man who has forgotten God. His heart is hard. He is a carnal man, fallen and low, and the earth shuts completely around him.

This is not the exceptional case—this is more likely to be the rule. How many in our day are aware that there is this hard crust that is over our hearts, our beings—and yet can never face it and confess it!

Everyone who has come to the years of responsibility seems to have gone on the defensive. Even some of you who have known me for years are surely on the defensive—you have your guard up all the time!

I know that you are not afraid of me, but you are afraid, nevertheless, of what I am going to say. Probably every faithful preacher today is fencing with masters as he faces his congregation. The guard is always up. The quick parry is always ready.

Guard completely down

It is very hard for me to accept the fact that it is now very rare for anyone to come into the house of God with guard completely down, head bowed and with the silent confession: "Dear Lord, I am ready and willing to hear what You will speak to my heart today!"

We have become so learned and so worldly and so sophisticated and so blasé and so bored and so religiously tired that the clouds of glory seem to have gone from us.

The very fact that I should have to talk like this is incriminating in itself: incriminating that a verse like this should not bring a fresh and instant response in the human breast when it is read.

God sent His Son into the world. He did not send Him to condemn. He sent Him that the world might be saved!

I ask again: how can we consider it with such indifference?

Brethren, who has poisoned our cup?

What evil alliances have we made?

What has sin been doing to our hearts?

What devil has been working on the strings of the harp of our soul?

Who has been giving us sedatives and feeding us the medicine of apathy?

What has happened to us that we can talk about this, sing about this, and even preach about this—and still be left untouched and unmoved?

Wordsworth was not a preacher but he sounded these same unanswered questions in his day when he wrote with honesty in his own soul: "I would rather be a heathen and believe in an outworn, heathen creed, standing on the shore of the ocean and imagining that I could hear old Neptune or old Triton blow his horn, than to be a civilized Christian within whom everything has died."

We live in a day of temptations, and the world is too much with us, getting and spending. But even for our kind of world, even for the human race in its present condition, there is no message, no hope, no word of authority and promise that can compare to God's proclamation of love and forgiveness.

There may be a time way out yonder in the glorious tomorrow when all that we know today is over and sin has passed away and the shadows have been driven from the sun and the brows of men are no longer furrowed, that there will be other and newer and grander proclamations that God may make based upon this one. But for us in our present condition there is no other proclamation as great as this.

Now, when the Word says that God sent His Son into the world, it is not talking to us merely about the world as geography. It does not just indicate to us that God sent His Son into the Near East, that He sent Him to Bethlehem in Palestine.

He came to Bethlehem, certainly. He did come to that little land that lies between the seas. But this message does not have any geographical or astronomical meaning. It has nothing to do with kilometers and distances and continents and mountains and towns.

What it really means is that God sent His Son into the human race. When it speaks of the world here, it does not mean that God just loved our geography. It does not mean that God so loved the snow-capped mountains or the sun-kissed meadows or the flowing streams or the great peaks of the north.

God may love all of these. I think He does. You cannot read the Book of Job or the Psalms without knowing that God is in love with the world He made.

He came to people

But that is not the meaning in this passage. God sent His Son to the human race. He came to people. This is something we must never forget—Jesus Christ came to seek and to save people. Not just certain favored people. Not just certain kinds of people. Not just people in general.

We humans do have a tendency to use generic terms and general terms and pretty soon we become just scientific in our outlook. Let us cast that outlook aside and confess that God loved each of us in a special kind of way so that His Son came into and unto and upon the people of the world—and He even became one of those people!

If you could imagine yourself to be like Puck and able to draw a ring around the earth in forty winks, just think of the kinds of people you would see all at once. You would see the crippled and the blind and the leprous. You would see the fat, the lean, the tall and the short. You would see the dirty and the clean. You would see some walking safely along the avenues with no fear of a policeman but you would see also those who skulk in back alleys and crawl through broken windows. You would see those who are healthy and you would see others twitching and twisting in the last agonies of death. You would see the ignorant and the illiterate as well as those gathered under the elms in some college town, nurturing deep dreams of great poems or plays or books to astonish and delight the world.

People! You would see the millions of people: people whose eyes slant differently from yours and people whose hair is not like your hair.

Their customs are not the same as yours, their habits are not the same. But they are all people. The thing is, their differences are all external. Their similarities are all within their natures. Their differences have to do with customs and habits. Their likeness has to do with nature.

Brethren, let us treasure this: God sent His Son to the people. He is the people's Savior. Jesus Christ came to give life and hope to people like your family and like mine.

The Savior of the world knows the true value and worth of every living soul. He pays no attention to status or human honor or class. Our Lord knows nothing about this status business that everyone talks about.

When Jesus came to this world, He never asked anyone, "What is your IQ?" He never asked anyone whether or not they were well-traveled. Let us thank God that He sent Him—and that He came! Both of those things are true. They are not contradictory. God sent Him as Savior! Christ, the Son, came to seek and to save! He came because He was sent and He came because His great heart urged Him and compelled Him to come. Now, let's think about the mission on which He came. Do you know what I have been thinking about our situation as people, as humans?

Let us think and imagine ourselves back to the condition of paganism. Let us imagine that we have no Bible and no hymn book and that these 2,000 years of Christian teaching and tradition had never taken place. We are on our own, humanly speaking.

Suddenly, someone arrives with a proclamation: "God is sending His Son into the human race. He is coming!"

What would be the first thing that we would think of? What would our hearts and consciences tell us immediately? We would run for the trees and rocks and hide like Adam among the trees of the Garden.

What would be the logical mission upon which God would send His Son into the world? We know what our nature is and we know that God knows all about us and He is sending His Son to face us.

Why would the Son of God come to our race?

Our own hearts—sin and darkness and deception and moral disease tell us what His mission should be. The sin we cannot deny tells us that He might have come to judge the world!

Why did the Holy Ghost bring this proclamation and word from God that "For God sent not his Son into the world to condemn the world" (John 3:17)?

Men and women are condemned in their own hearts because they know that if the Righteous One is coming, then we ought to be sentenced.

But God had a greater and far more gracious purpose—He came that sinful men might be saved. The loving mission of our Lord Jesus Christ was not to condemn but to forgive and reclaim.

Why did He come to men and not to fallen angels? Well, I have said this before in this pulpit, and I could be right although many seem to think that because others are not saying it I must be wrong: I believe He came to men and not to angels because man at the first was created in the image of God and angels were not. I believe He came to fallen Adam's brood and not to fallen devils because the fallen brood of Adam had once borne the very image of God.

Morally logical decision

Thus, I believe it was a morally logical decision, that when Jesus Christ became incarnate it was in the flesh and body of a man because God had made man in His image.

I believe that although man was fallen and lost and on his way to hell, he still had a capacity and potential that made the Incarnation possible, so that God Almighty could pull up the blankets of human flesh around His ears and become a Man to walk among men.

There was nothing of like kind among angels and fallen creatures—so He came not to condemn but to reclaim and to restore and to regenerate.

We have been trying to think of this condescension of God in personal and individual terms and what it should mean to each one of us to be loved of God in this way.

Now I think I hear someone saying, "But John 3:16 does not mention the cross. You have been telling about God's love but you have not mentioned the cross and His death on our behalf!"

Just let me say that there are some who insist and imagine that whenever we preach we should just open our mouths and in one great big round paragraph include every bit of theology there is to preach.

John 3:16 does not mention the cross and I declare to you that God is not nearly as provincial as we humans are. He has revealed it all and has included it all and has said it all somewhere in the Book, so that the cross stands out like a great, bright, shining pillar in the midst of the Scriptures.

We remember, too, that without the cross on which the Savior died there could be no Scriptures, no revelation, no redemptive message, nothing! But here He gave us a loving proclamation—He sent His Son; He gave His Son! Then later it develops that in giving His Son, He gave Him to die!

I have said that this must be a personal word for every man and every woman. Like a prodigal son in that most moving of all stories, each one of us must come to grips with our own personal need and to decide and act as he did: "I perish with hunger. I will arise and go to my father." (Luke 15:17–18). He said, "I will arise"—so he got up and went to his father.

You must think of yourself—for God sent His Son into the world to save you!

Here I insist that you must have some faith about yourself and I am almost afraid to say it because someone will send me a critical, nagging letter.

I am not asking you to have faith *in* yourself—I am only insisting that it is right for you to show faith *about* yourself, faith in Christ and in what He has promised you as an individual person.

That is, you must believe that you are the one He meant when He said, "Come home."

Believe he meant you

All of the general faith you have about God will not do you any good at all unless you are willing to believe that He meant you—you yourself—when He said "God so loves that He gave His Son for you!"

The prodigal son could have said in general terms: "When one is hungry and ready to perish, one could return to his father's house." But he said, "I am the one that is hungry. I am the one for whom my father has a complete provision. I will arise and go!"

God lovingly waits for each individual to come with a personal resolve and decision: "I will arise and I will go home to claim the provision in my Father's house." If you will make that personal decision of faith in Jesus Christ, with faith in the fact that it is really you whom God loves and wants to forgive, it will mean something more to you than you have ever known—something beautiful and eternal.

I close by reminding you also as an individual that unbelief always finds three trees behind which to hesitate and hide. Here they are: Somebody Else. Some Other Place. Some Other Time.

We hear someone preaching an invitation sermon on John 3:16 and in effect we run to the garden to hide behind these trees.

"Of course it is true," we say, "but it is for Somebody Else."

If it were only Some Other Place or at Some Other Time you might be willing to come.

Whether you get the right grammar or the proper tense is not important: what our Lord is delighted to hear is your confession that "that means me, Lord! I am the reason, the cause and reason why You came to earth to die."

That is positive, personal faith in a personal Redeemer—and that is what saves you. I give you my word that if you will just rush in there, just as you are and with faith in Jesus Christ, our Lord has very little concern as to whether or not you know all of the theology in the world!

The Divine Appointment

*There was a man sent from God . . . to bear wit-
ness of the Light . . .* (John 1:6-7)

I confess that I find myself coming back often to
the message and the ministry of John the Baptist, for the Bible record is very plain that this man
John was *a man sent from God.*

Looking into the Scripture, I do not think we
would be challenged if we said that John the Baptist was the greatest of all the prophets. Our Lord
Jesus Christ made a very plain and revealing assessment of the greatness of this John in Luke
7:28: "For I say unto you, Among those that are
born of women there is not a greater prophet than
John the Baptist: but he that is least in the kingdom of God is greater than he."

I cannot refrain from asking you a question
here: How do you suppose the Christian church,

as we know it today, would be inclined to deal with John the Baptist if he came into our scene?

Our generation would probably decide that such a man ought to be downright proud of the fact that God had sent him. We would urge him to write books and make a documentary film and the seminary leaders would line up to schedule him as guest lecturer.

But in that distant generation of mankind to whom the eternal Son of God presented Himself as suffering Savior and living Lord, John the Baptist gladly stepped down—allowing Jesus the Christ to displace him completely.

This was his example: instead of insisting on recognition as a man sent from God, he pointed to Jesus as the true Light and said in genuine humility, "I am not worthy to unloose his shoe's latchet" (see John 1:27).

That was John, and when his ministry was over, Jesus came. It was then that John said to all who would listen, "Behold the Lamb of God" (1:29). He directed all the eyes away from himself to Jesus. And then? John the Baptist just faded out of the picture.

Actually, John the Baptist would never have fit into the contemporary religious scene in our day—never! He did not keep his suit pressed. He was not careful about choosing words that would not offend anyone. Something tells me that John the Baptist did not quote beautiful passages from the poets.

Adjusted to the times

Some of the doctors of psychiatry in our day would have had quick advice for John the Baptist: "John, we have been observing you and the way you live and the way you talk and the way you dress. John, you really ought to get adjusted to the times and to society!"

I will just put in a thought for myself here. If a doctor ever checks me over and tells me that I need to "get adjusted," I will just grab my hat and leave. I am not a machine and I do not need to have anyone trying to adjust me.

Adjust—that is one of the modern words I have come to hate. It never was an expression in the language used to speak about human beings until we forgot that we have a soul and began to think of ourselves only in materialistic terms. Then when men like John B. Watson began to say that besides not having a soul, man also really does not have a mind, actually doing his thinking with his gut muscle, the need for personal adjustment was explained to us. Since then we have had weird guys with mental "screwdrivers" adjusting this person a little tighter and adjusting that one a little looser.

My brethren, John the Baptist did not invite adjustment—he preached repentance.

John the Baptist did not invite people to sit down with him in order to engage in religious speculation. The Baptist was not afraid to preach about sin, and he knew that religious speculation is an evil because it leaves sin in the life completely undisturbed.

Religious speculation never deals with the self-sins—those hyphenated, little two-part devils that eat at the vitals of men. They are self-love and self-righteousness and self-admiration and self-esteem and a hundred other such self-sins that lie within man's being.

I remember hearing about a Chinese boy who was learning the English language and he had trouble with certain words and phrases. Asked if he could cook eggs, he gave a proud reply in his English: "I can fry them or I can disturb them."

Well, the scrambled egg is a disturbed egg. We admit that. Our human trouble is that we can talk for years about religion without having any inward conviction or disturbance. We never allow God to "scramble" us, to get hold of our hearts and bother us about our sin. We find it very hard to take the lid off and allow God to see deep inside of us.

John the Baptist proclaimed a straight, spiritual message and he preached for decisions and for results. I am confident that at no point in his ministry did he ever invite a group of inquirers to come together for a discussion session about their problems.

Now, this of course gives me opportunity to assume one of those radical positions which I am always supposed to be taking. I may as well play in character because I do take it.

A religion of discussion groups

I am greatly bothered about Christianity becoming a religion of discussion groups. The trouble is that people in our day like to come together to discuss religion, but not to repent.

I would not give you 50 cents a group for all of the religious discussions that are scheduled throughout this entire year. You have a moderator and he wants to know what everyone thinks and when it is all over we have just been playing a game. We have been batting the shuttlecock back and forth across the court but we have not gotten through to our hearts.

It is my opinion that five minutes on your knees with God in complete sincerity will get you closer to the Lord and closer to the truth than all of the discussion groups in the world. The farther we get from the cross and the farther we get from repentance, the more we run to panel groups and discussions.

I believe the Lord will forgive me—for I have taken part in some of them myself. I want to testify right now and report that no one ever got anything out of it!

I hope you will just take it for what it is worth. If someone suggests that you discuss religion with them, I recommend that you say, "Let's pray!"

I know that when people used to come to Dr. A.B. Simpson and ask: "Dr. Simpson, just what do you mean by this or that teaching?" he would often respond, "Let us just bow our heads. We are going to pray together." That usually ended the discussion because you cannot very well argue with a godly old man who is pouring out his heart to God in your presence.

Oh brethren, how much we could learn from the life and ministry of John the Baptist if we were willing to be disturbed, willing for God to put spiritual desire in our hearts.

It is certain that the greatness of this man John did not lie within himself and within his own capabilities. His greatness lay in his high office and in his high privilege as a man actually sent from God. John's office was bigger than John because of what God was doing in the fullness of time.

On the other hand, Elijah was bigger than his office for he had no position, really. It is not difficult to be bigger than a position that you do not have.

You may think that both you and I are confused at this point, but I think it will be clear as we go on.

The Bible record tells us that Abraham saw our Lord's day and was glad. But John the Baptist actually lived in our Lord's day and that made him greater than Abraham.

David played his harp and sang of the coming of One who would be wounded and pierced, yet would rise and sing among His brethren. But John the Baptist was there when He came. He saw Him and knew Him.

Isaiah prophesied of the One who should come, born of a virgin; One who should eat butter and honey and should grow up as a root out of the dry ground. But John the Baptist recognized Him and touched Him and baptized Him. His privilege was the greater.

Reasons John was greater

Malachi said He would suddenly come into His temple and sit as a purifier of silver, but John the Baptist actually walked in that temple. We may give an application of Malachi's vision of One to come as a reference to the second return of Christ, yet that same purifier of silver was there and John saw Him and recognized Him and, in a sense, inaugurated Him into His earthly ministry.

There are good reasons why I say that the privilege of John was greater than that of any of the others among men.

The first rests upon the fact that John was indeed a man sent from God. The writers Matthew and Mark tell about John the Baptist, but they give us no pedigree. Luke writes about him, giving us his family history, telling who his parents were, as well as the wonder of his birth.

But John presses in farther, rising higher as John always seems to do, penetrating through to the essential greatness of the Baptist as a man sent from God. The evangelist had special discernment and penetration of vision. Others might say of John the Baptist that he was the greatest, that he was the wisest, that he was the strongest or that he was the most eloquent.

But the Apostle John witnesses that this was John's greatness—he was a man sent from God!

In this, I say, he took note of the real mark of excellence, for John the Baptist could not have had any higher honor. For John it was not only an un-

speakably high honor, but for the world it consti-
tuted a treasure, as well.

You know that I am never through talking to
you about using the mind God has given you. Do
you ever just get away by yourself to think and
meditate on some of the wonders of God?

When I am on trains or waiting in a station I notice that many people spend their spare time with
crossword puzzles. Many of them look as if they
are bright but I doubt if they are if I am to judge by
what they are doing with their time.

Now, I don't want you to get mad at me. If you
really like crossword puzzles I guess it is all right. I
guess it is all right, too, if you want to suck your
thumb. My point is that there is something we can
do with our time and with our minds that is a
whole lot better than crossword puzzles.

I recommend as a mental exercise that you try to
think what the world would be like today if John
the Baptist had never lived and ministered. Then go
on and try to think what the world would be like if
your Lord Jesus had never come to dwell in our
midst. Think what the world would be today if
there were no church of the firstborn.

Think them all out of the world—and then try
to piece the world together without them. I assure
you it will be an exercise in history and in spiritual
values that will infinitely exceed any puzzles you
might ever hope to complete.

What I am saying is that the coming of John the
Baptist, the sending of this man from God, was an

inestimable blessing, an unspeakable treasure to the world.

Oh, God sends forth His men, honoring the world as He does so, but also providing an example and a spiritual lesson for all men. I believe this; I have always believed this.

You cannot deny that the life and vitality of the Christian church lie in the spiritual leadership of men anointed of the Holy Ghost. I dare to tell you that there is danger in too much democracy in the life of the church.

I am sure that some of you with a strong Baptist background will curl up like a burning leaf in the autumn to hear me say this, but that is all right: I am half Baptist myself!

But I do not believe that God expects the Christian church to thrive and mature and grow just on plain democratic principles. If you will check around you will find that even those who hold to democracy in their church policy never get beyond first base unless they have leaders within the denomination who are anointed men, strongly spiritual in leadership.

There was a man sent from God whose name was Noah. A just man, Noah builded himself an ark and saved himself and his wife and eight persons, saving the human race from extinction.

There was a man sent from God whose name was Abraham. He came from Ur of the Chaldees, following nothing but the light in his own heart and the dimly seen vision of the living God. Abraham became the founder of the Jewish nation.

There was a man sent from God named Moses, who took a nation lost in darkness and bondage in Egypt through the miracle of the Red Sea and into the wilderness, where he guided and cherished and nursed and cared for it through forty years.

When Moses died, God sent a man whose name was Joshua, who gathered the nation as a hen gathers her chicks and established Israel in the land that God had promised to Abraham, Isaac and Jacob.

There was a man sent from God whose name was David and he reached into his own heart and tore out the sounding strings and set those strings in the windows of the synagogues for a thousand years so that the winds of persecution blew across them, making music for the Jewish worshipers.

When the veil of the temple was rent and the Holy Ghost had come, those same harp strings taken from the heart of David were strung in the windows of the churches; so today in our churches we cannot sing without having David sing also. In a very true sense, the man sent from God whose name was David taught the world to sing, and we have been singing David's songs ever since.

Oh, there was a man sent from God whose name was Paul, and another man whose name was Peter. And many centuries later when the church had been buried under the debris and settlings of the dust of Romanism, there was a man sent from God whose name was Luther, and he feared no one. He brought back the Bible again, translating it into sonorous and musical German.

There was a man sent from God whose name was Simpson and he was joined by another whose name was Jaffray, and they combined in praying and taking the Christian gospel to great unreached sections of our world in the past generation. Go down the line—take any list you happen to be fond of and wherever men had done great things for God, they have been men who were sent from God.

Secular honors

In our human society we give honors to many men and women for noble things that they do.

There is no doubt that Winston Churchill played a most important part in turning back Hitler and his hordes in the great war, and perhaps saving the western world from extinction. As a result, he was called Sir Winston for the rest of his life.

He had an important mission, but I do not think that anyone ever suggested that Sir Winston was sent from God.

I think of another great Englishman and I think it could be said of him that there was a man sent from God whose name was John Wesley. When the records are all written and the angel of God has graded them and approved them, I am confident that the man sent from God whose name was Wesley will take his place high above the man who was sent by the government of Britain, great statesman though he may have been.

I hope our young people never forget the true estimate of honors and of values. Young man, the president of the United States could call you to Washington, commission you as an ambassador of your country and send you off on important missions to other nations—but how much greater for you to be owned and commissioned and empowered and sent from God on His business and for His glory.

No king and no president has authority and power enough to bestow that greatest of all honors—to be owned and honored and sent from God!

You young people, with your energy and enthusiasm and potential, I plead with you—get your values right and get your ambitions right and take great care before you pick anyone for your life's example.

God Almighty has meant for us to sail high and far with purest motives—and we just settle for lesser things. How sad that we who are provided with a kind of heavenly propulsion, aiming at the stars and planets, should so prostitute our ambitions that we burn out and come down with a thud only a little way over in a rice paddy. Remember that the honors God gives are the eternal and unfading honors!

Why John was honored

Let me give you some reasons why I believe God could honor John the Baptist in that day in which he lived.

First, John had the ability to live and meditate in solitude. He knew the meaning of quietness. He was in the desert until the time of his showing forth unto Israel as a prophet. He came out of his lonely solitude to break the silence like a drumbeat or as the trumpet sounds. The crowds came—all gathered to hear this man who had been with God and who had come from God.

In our day we just cannot get quiet enough and serene enough to wait on God. Somebody has to be talking. Somebody has to be making noise. But John had gone into the silence and had matured in a kind of special school with God and the stars and the wind and the sand.

I think it is really true that the more understanding we have within our own beings, the less need we have of people all around us. If you do not have anything inside, you must compensate for your inner vacuity by surrounding yourself with social noisemakers. A lot of people live like that. They have never practiced the art of quietness, of holy solitude.

John the Baptist probably did not have good manners and he was unaware of all the social niceties—but he had met God in the silence. I do not believe it is stretching a point at all to say that we will most often hear from God in those times when we are silent.

The abrasive action of society has taken the character out of many a man and has reduced him to be just one more thin, shiny dime among all the dimes of the world, shiny from much use and many contacts. He has lost all his milling, his design. He has lost all of his proper characteristics.

I am not impressed by the active, frenetic soulwinner who has to get out where the action is and "make some contacts for Jesus!"

Brother, just get alone with Jesus for a while; let your two knees make contact with the ground and do not be afraid or ashamed to stay there for a while. John the Baptist could be sent of God; he had the proper training somewhere in the quiet presence of his God.

John had a second attribute that was blessed of God, and that was his simplicity. He was satisfied to be simple in dress and in diet. He was simple in his faith in God. He was not trying to impress anyone.

A friend was telling me about being in a meeting of religious men and one of those present got up and said, "What this denomination needs to do is to get out and begin bragging about ourselves!"

Oh, brag about ourselves, indeed! Just as soon as we get such ideas in our relationships with God, He washes His hands of the whole mess. I can just hear Him: "That bunch of braggers. I will have nothing to do with them!"

Well, John the Baptist was sent from God and he did not spend any of his time bragging. He just walked around simply doing the will of God.

Another thing that John the Baptist possessed was the right kind of vision, a true spiritual discernment. He could see things as they were.

The Holy Spirit came like a dove, descended like a dove, putting down his pink feet and disappearing into the heart of the Son of God.

I wonder out of all those crowds who saw the Holy Ghost come?

Only John the Baptist. I do not think anyone else had the kind of vision that was necessary to see Him.

You know I am not talking about magic; I am talking about a divine revelation for a specific cause, a specific reason.

John said, "And I knew him not: but he that sent me to baptize with water, the same said unto me, Upon whom thou shalt see the Spirit descending, and remaining on him, the same is he which baptizeth with the Holy Ghost" (John 1:33).

John the Baptist was a man of vision in the midst of men who had no vision. He knew where he was in his times. The drift of the hour or the trend of the times in religion would never carry him away.

John had courage

Now, one more thought and that is about courage. John had it; he stood there and said to the religious leaders of his day, "O generation of vipers" (Luke 3:7).

No poetry there, brother. No religious accommodation there.

When I meet some of the Christians of our day who apparently do not have the courage to meet a real live mouse head on, I conclude that not many of us will be "sent from God." We do not have the courage to be different. We do not have the courage to risk losing something—for Jesus' sake.

What kind of Christians and what kind of preachers are we in these days? Afraid that we will lose our reputation. Afraid that we will lose public esteem and be criticized. Afraid we will lose our influence, or "pull." Afraid we will lose our friends.

Let me give you some spiritual advice about spiritual courage. God Almighty has called us to be His sheep; and He has made no mention of mice, at all.

There are exceptions to every rule, and the figure of sheep just does not hold up when it comes to prophets and soldiers and warriors in a day of declension and sin.

Therefore, it does not surprise me at all when God sometimes straps the shield and buckler on one of His sheep and stands him up on his two hind legs and by His own kind of miracle changes him from being a sheep into being a roaring lion. That is how God gets Himself a John the Baptist or a Martin Luther or a Charles Finney.

Well, brethren, John the Baptist did not want anything for himself. He just wanted to live to glorify His God. He admitted that he was not the bridegroom: "Just to be present and hear the voice of the bridegroom is all I want."

I do not need to remind you that the God of John is still the God of this hour. Nothing has been changed and He is still seeking men and women in whom He can find those characteristics that marked John the Baptist.

That does not mean that we must go back into the woods and eat locusts and wild honey and do away with education. That would be foolish.

But it is within our hearts and our beings that God searches and looks. It is our spiritual heart life that is to be simple. It is in our hearts that we are to meditate and be silent. It is deep within our beings that we must be courageous and open to God's leadings.

If there ever was an hour in which the church needed courageous men of prophetic vision, it is now. Preachers and pastors? They can be turned out in our schools like automobiles off the assembly line.

But prophets? Where are they?

The simple, humble and courageous men who are willing to serve and wait on God in the long silences, who wait to hear what God says before they go to tell the world—these do not come along too often. When they do, they seek only to glorify their God and His Christ!

The Essence
of Faith

*Nicodemus answered and said unto him, How
can these things be?* (John 3:9)

We have every indication in the Scriptures that the account of Nicodemus seeking out our Lord Jesus Christ prior to His death and resurrection is of great importance in the realm of the Christian faith.

Out of the billions of people who have lived in the world, out of the millions of Jews who have lived in the world, and out of the tens of thousands who were part of the tradition of the Pharisees, the Holy Spirit has seen fit to let a penetrating pencil of light fall upon the head of one man—Nicodemus, the Pharisee of Israel.

We have come to understand that the Holy Spirit of God is rigidly economical in the use of words in the divine revelation. Through John, the Holy Spirit has devoted a total of twenty-one verses to this story of Nicodemus visiting Jesus; we learn what he said to Christ and what Christ said to him.

This, without any other consideration, would lead us to believe that this is a story of great importance. If it were not important, God would never have put it in the record at all.

Therefore, we want to approach it respectfully, reverently, and with an inquiring mind.

Let us consider this man Nicodemus within the context of his own day and time. He was a Pharisee. He was a member of the strictest sect in the religious life of Israel. He was a fundamentalist par excellence, following Judaism in its strictest and straightest interpretations of the letter of the law.

Also, we are made aware that Nicodemus was a ruler in Israel, being one of the seventy members of the powerful Sanhedrin, a tribunal not quite equivalent to our own Supreme Court, but very much like it, with some executive as well as judicial authority.

Members of the Sanhedrin were from the privileged families of Israel. The high priest was the president. Former high priests still living were members. Some elders and legal assessors were members, along with powerful scribes of the day. It is interesting, too, that members of the Sanhedrin could be either Pharisees or Sadducees, which coincides in a sense with the fact that Supreme Court justices in our own day may be either Republican or Democrat.

The Bible record plainly tells us that only one of the seventy members of the Sanhedrin at that time bothered to seek an interview with Jesus of Nazareth, and that was Nicodemus. He crossed over the great gulf that separated them in that day.

Does this tell us anything about the essence of faith?

Nicodemus came to Jesus by night, evidently feeling his way. He surely knew something about what it would cost him to show any serious interest in the person or the ministry of this Jesus of Nazareth.

He knew that the disciples of Jesus had abandoned all, left all behind. Their faith in His cause did not come without costing each of them something.

"It will cost you nothing!"

In our day, there is a tendency for enthusiastic Christian promoters to teach that the essence of faith is this: "Come to Jesus—it will cost you nothing! The price has all been paid—it will cost you nothing!"

Brethren, that is a dangerous half-truth. There is always a price connected with salvation and with discipleship.

But some will say: "Isn't that what the mission-aries teach all around the world? Don't they say, 'Come! Everything is free. Jesus paid it all'?"

God's grace is free, no doubt about that. No one in the wide world can make any human payment towards the plea of salvation or the forgiveness of sins.

But I know the missionaries well enough to know that they would never go to people any-where in the world and simply teach: "You do not have to do a thing. Your faith in Jesus Christ will never cost you anything."

I have been receiving a magazine in the mail—someone sends it to me in a plain wrapper with no return address. I wish he or she would stop sending it.

The man who edits this paper also preaches on the radio and the philosophy he spreads is this: "Everybody in the world has faith. All you have to do is turn your faith loose in the right direction. Turn it towards Christ and everything is all fixed up!"

Now, that is truly a misconception of what the Bible says about man and about God and about faith. It is a misconception fostered by the devil himself.

The Apostle Paul told believers plainly and clearly that "not everyone has faith."

Actually, faith is a rare plant. Faith is not a plant that grows everywhere by the way. It is not a common plant that belongs to everyone. Faith is a rare and wonderful plant that lives and grows only in the penitent soul.

The teaching that everyone has faith and all you have to do is use it is simply a form of humanism in the guise of Christianity. I warn you that any faith that belongs to everybody is a humanistic faith and it is not the faith that saves. It is not that faith which is a gift of God to a broken heart.

I think it must be apparent to us that Nicodemus, a ruler in Israel, would have known what it might cost him to inquire of Jesus about the things of faith and of God's plan and of eternal life. He was feeling his way.

What the scholars say

I share with you here some of the research and some of the speculations which scholars and writers have given us concerning those years in history following the death and resurrection of Christ.

You should understand that there is a question mark after these historical speculations, but we should know what scholars suggest.

Some scholars believe that this Nicodemus was Nicodemus Ben Gorian, a brother of the celebrated Jewish historian, Flavius Josephus. This Nicodemus was said to be one of the three richest men in Jerusalem at that time.

Whether history or legend, the story passed down through the centuries tells us that the daughter of Nicodemus Ben Gorian was reduced to picking up corn or grain off the streets of Jerusalem, where it had been thrown from the feed bags of horses as they traveled down the street. She picked up what she could in order to roast it and have something to eat.

Why was the daughter of one of Jerusalem's most wealthy men reduced to such a state of hunger?

The historians suggest at least that when Nicodemus finally threw in his lot with Jesus the Christ, he was stripped by the ruling society of all that he had. His property was confiscated and he was turned out as if he were the scum of the earth.

It is plain enough that Nicodemus came to Jesus by night—and that has resulted in a great deal of abuse being heaped on his memory throughout the centuries. But he came feeling his way. He came inquiring. He came asking questions. From our vantage point in time, we believe that he was spiritually sensitive and that he was seeking answers about the things of God which he himself did not know.

Let me tell you what his coming to Jesus suggests to me. It suggests that the soul of man is too nobly conceived and too highly born and too mighty and mysterious a universe in itself ever to be satisfied with anything less than Jesus the Christ, the eternal Son of God.

His coming to Jesus suggests that only Jesus Christ is enough; only in Jesus Christ are there adequate answers to the questions men have always asked about God and eternity, of life, forgiveness and blessing.

I can stand and assure you without any embarrassment that no matter who you are, either now or later in your life or at death or in the world to come, you will find that only Jesus Christ is enough.

Now, as far as we know, of the total of seventy ruling men in the Sanhedrin at the time we are speaking of, only one crossed over and came to Jesus asking questions about eternal life and the kingdom of God.

Why was Nicodemus that one? He was separated from Jesus Christ by the same wide gulf of religious tradition and practice that separated Jesus from the other sixty-nine rulers in Israel.

Nicodemus was in a high ruling position and Jesus was a common carpenter turned teacher.

By their very nature, men of the Sanhedrin majored in religious bigotry while Jesus surely was anything but a straight-laced bigot. The religious philosophy of Jesus was as broad as all of Palestine and to that you could add the Mediterranean also.

Beside the pride of high position, Nicodemus would have inherited the sharp prejudice that every educated Jewish member of the ruling Sanhedrin would feel for lowly carpenters and unschooled fishermen.

Why would Nicodemus knowingly seek to cross that gulf?

What mysterious power could lay hold of the mind and conscience of the man Nicodemus and none of the other sixty-nine?

Could it be that as a man, he was simply more sensitive to the voice of God and the inner strivings of God in his being?

You have heard me speak quite often about the prevenient grace of God—that mysterious, secret working of God in the souls of men; turning them toward Himself, influencing them toward Himself and magnetically attracting them to Himself.

It is surely true that if it were not for the prevenient work that God does within the hearts of men and women there could never be a conversion. So I wonder if this man Nicodemus was simply more sensitive to this operation of God than the other sixty-nine.

Oh, you think that God picked out Nicodemus, selected him alone and let the other sixty-nine go?

No one, not even in 1,000 years of jumping up and down on the family Bible, could ever make me believe that God showed anything like partiality. The heart of God that yearned over Nicodemus yearned over the rest of those men in the Sanhedrin.

Sensitivity to God's voice

But only Nicodemus came—and I think it was because he was more sensitive to God's voice and God's Spirit.

We have the same conditions in our churches today. I am talking to some of you right now who have been reared in Christian homes. You have been brought up in the Sunday school. You cut your first baby tooth on the back of a hymnal when your mother was not watching.

Still, to this day, you are not right with God. Some of you have made a kind of halfway profession but you have never been able to delight yourself in the Lord. The reason is that you lack sensitivity to the voice of God and you could not care less about the will of God. If the voice and the concern of the Spirit of God does not move something within your own spirit every day, you are not going to be much of a Christian—if you are a Christian at all!

I think Nicodemus had a sensitivity within his own spirit that caused him to move and to act and to inquire. I think he must have been more receptive to spiritual impulses than other leaders among the Jews in their day.

Consider this man: although he was a strict Pharisee, a member of the Sanhedrin, cursed we might say with the pride of high position and religious prejudice and bigotry, he still revealed a receptivity to spiritual impulses.

Brethren, I don't mind telling you that I want to keep that kind of spiritual receptivity alive within my own soul.

I would rather lose a leg and hobble along throughout the rest of my life than to lose my sensitivity to God and to His voice and to spiritual things. Oh, I want to keep that within me, within my soul!

I believe something else about this man Nicodemus: he must have possessed a basic humility that others did not have.

I caution you that there are many people among us who are not ever going to get right with God, and the reason is that they simply will not humble themselves, ever!

Some cannot even humble themselves enough to go to church where the preaching is plain and the gospel is narrow. We know about that here—in this particular church. We have a good reputation—we pay our bills on time and we help people who are in need, and not many go to jail from this church.

But in spite of that, many on the outside think that we are eccentric, a little bit off center, too dogmatic where the things of God are concerned. You know, it takes some humility to cast in your lot with people who are serious enough about spiritual priorities that it causes those on the outside to feel that we must be in need of psychiatric help.

Well, I remind you that our Lord Jesus had that kind of a crowd around Him all the time. He was considered to be a very strange kind of man in His time—so those who gave up all to follow Him were also thought to be very strange.

I think Nicodemus must have had some gracious sense of humility to come to Jesus.

Human pride

Actually, pride is an awesome quality in mankind; not only in Jesus' day but in ours as well.

As an example, I heard a newscast in which one of India's highest officials was trying to apologize to the world about an international report that Christian missionaries were being hindered in their work in India.

"I want you to know that the report is not true," he said. "We are not hindering the propagation of the Christian doctrine in India. In fact, we understand that there have actually been a few people of low caste who have believed the Christian teaching."

Oh, the rising pride that must have been in that official's voice as he made his statement. The helpless and the hopeless in the lowest caste of his country—he was not going to get in their way if they wanted to believe in Jesus Christ.

The bigotry of human pride—you will find it everywhere in the world. It feasts on almost anything that will make it fat!

Against this background of the visit by Nicodemus, I would like to consider with you the example of several others who came to Jesus from various levels of life and culture.

There was the rich young ruler and everyone who has read the Bible will remember him, for he is considered by so many to have been an example of the model man.

He had four things going for him, things that everyone might want to emulate and possess. He had wealth and morality, position and youth.

I can just hear the mothers in Israel holding up this man as an example for their own children: "If you want to be like someone in particular, choose this rich young fellow as your example!"

In the minds of most people, they are sure that they would be enjoying peace of mind if only they were young, wealthy, of high position and living with good moral standards.

But when this young ruler came to Jesus, his very first question gave the clue to his own dissatisfaction in life: "What good thing shall I do, that I may have eternal life?" (Matthew 19:16).

He was young but he knew that he looked forward to a day when he would be withered and palsied and shaking with age, and that ultimately he would lie down stiffly on the bed from which he would never rise again.

He knew also that his wealth could not help him then. He knew that he would lose his position and his place would be filled by another. Even his morality was not sufficient answer for the life to come.

He realized that he had to discover and find out about something with eternity in it.

Brethren, let me say that until we are really converted to Christ and the holiness of Christ enters our hearts and lives, we are all part and parcel of a mighty deception: we are called upon to pretend that we can have peace of mind within and that we can be relatively happy and make a big success of our human lives if we have youth and wealth and morality and high position.

In that sense of what is going on all around us, David never had to apologize for writing that "all men are liars" (Psalm 116:11).

This whole human concept of success and happiness and inner peace based upon who we are and what we have is completely false, just as the rich young ruler found out.

The word eternal
The one important word is missing from it all, and that is the word *eternal*.

That young ruler knew, just as we all know, that there is not a person alive who has eternal youth, or eternal wealth; who has an eternal righteousness or an everlasting position or dominion.

The word *eternal* is not there. The rich young ruler found that within the will God had given him, he had to make a choice between things that pass away and those things that are of eternal value.

Think with me also of the Ethiopian chancellor whose story is in the eighth chapter of Acts.

Notice the things he could offer on the human side. He had great authority, plenty of prestige and an acquired religion. He had power and authority because of his position under the queen of Ethiopia. He was a Jewish proselyte, having gone through the religious rites that brought him into the Jewish religion.

He had come to Jerusalem to take part in one of the religious festivals of his new-found religion.

But he was a discriminating man, a thoughtful man, an unfulfilled man.

The swinging of the censers in ritual, the chanting of the priests, the majesty of the forms of worship—none of these made his own heart sing, none of these brought him to the point of rejoicing and gladness.

But when the evangelist Philip had preached Jesus to him, when he had met Jesus through active and saving faith, the Bible record tells us that he went on his way rejoicing.

Only Jesus, the Christ, the eternal Son of God, is enough. Man has to face up to the fact that religion is not enough—and it never will be.

Oh, it is amazing how many things religious people want to do to you. They can start when you are eight days old with circumcision and end up with the last rites when you are 108 years old—and all of that time they will be rubbing something on you, or putting something around your neck, or making you eat something or insisting that you should not eat something. They will manipulate you, maul you, and sweetly massage your soul all the time—and when it is all done you are just what you were. You are just a decorated and massaged sinner—a sinner who did not eat meat or on the other hand, a sinner who did eat fish.

When religion has done all it can, you are still a sinner who either went to the temple or did not go to the temple. If you attended church you are still a sinner who attended church. If you did not go to church you are still a sinner who did not go to church.

Measured in any direction and approached from any point of view, we are still sinners if all we have is that which religion has offered and tried to do for us. Religion can put us on the roll and educate us and train us and instruct us and discipline us; and when it is all over there is still something within our being that cries, "Eternity is in my heart and I have not found anything to satisfy it."

So, you will be searching and searching forever until you find Christ, for only Christ is enough to satisfy the eternal longing in our souls.

Now think with me, too, of Lydia, in Acts, chapter 16.

A career woman

Lydia was a career woman in her own right. I would say she was born out of due time, long before there were laws and amendments to set women free.

I have to tell the women of our day that we have set them free to be just as bad as the men—and just as miserable! We have set them free to curse and swear and tell dirty stories and smoke cigarettes. We have made them free to set their own morals, to make nasty political speeches and, of course, to vote as blindly as men do.

God knows that I cannot do anything about it, ladies. You just look at me and shrug; push past me and take my seat in the bus!

Well, Lydia was a woman who surely thought she had found freedom and satisfaction in that era when they did not count women at all; they just counted the men. She was a seller of purple. She traveled in the nations of that day. She should have been the happiest woman in all of Asia Minor.

In the city of Philippi, by the riverside where some women met on the Sabbath to pray, Lydia heard the Apostle Paul tell of the death and resurrection of the Lord Jesus Christ and the record shows that the Lord opened her heart. She gladly put her faith in Christ and was baptized.

She said humbly to Paul: "If ye have judged me to be faithful to the Lord, come into my house, and abide there" (Acts 16:15).

That was Lydia. She had found that her career and her freedom and her abilities lacked the word eternal. Now she had found the answer and the only answer in Jesus Christ, the eternal Son, the Savior.

Nathanael came to Jesus and he was an interesting case. The Bible record does not tell us too much about him—but I think it could well be said that he was a fellow full of prejudice like any other man on the street.

When Philip told him that the disciples had found the Messiah of whom the Old Testament had spoken, Nathanael gave his cynical reply: "Can there any good thing come out of Nazareth?" (John 1:46).

You see, Nathanael was a plain and simple man living from day to day, but he lived under the shadow of his humanness and he just could not get the sun to come out.

But when he came to Jesus and found that Jesus already knew him better than he knew himself, he was suddenly in the radiant sunlight and he confessed to Jesus, "Rabbi, thou art the Son of God; thou art the King of Israel" (1:49).

Truly, the way of man is not in himself, and that is what the Holy Ghost has said. Only Jesus Christ, the eternal Son, is enough.

We have asked why it was only Nicodemus who came. We could ask why Lydia's heart responded while many other women of her day felt no response to Christ's claims. Why did Nathanael respond to the appeal of Jesus on that day when so many others were either indifferent or filled with hatred?

I do believe in that secret and mysterious working of God in the human breast, deep within the beings of men and women.

I think the same questions could be raised of my testimony of finding the forgiving and converting grace of God in the Savior, Jesus Christ.

There was something in the line from which I came that was almost antireligion. Morality to a certain level—but not religious. Attitudes that were cold, earthy, profane. This I must say of both my father and my mother. High human standards, morality—but completely without any thought of God. God might as well not have existed. My parents appeared to be without a spark of desire after God.

Can you tell me why, then, at the age of seventeen, as a boy surrounded by unbelief, 100 percent, I could find my way to my mother's attic, kneel on my knees and give my heart and life in committal to Jesus Christ? Can you tell me how I could be thoroughly and completely converted without help from anyone on the outside? In my case when I came in faith to Jesus Christ there was not a single human being to help. There was nobody with a marked New Testament showing me how easy it is. There was no friend placing an arm over my shoulder to pray beside me.

I cannot answer the questions of "Why?" I can only testify that my conversion to Jesus Christ was as real as any man's conversion has ever been. You tell me why. I do not know why. I can only say that I know there is such a thing as the secret working of God in the human being who has a sensitivity to hear the call of God.

Oh, man—if you feel the tug of God in your breast, what a happy man you should be. What a marvelous and mysterious privilege if you feel the inner tug of God in your bosom and hear the secret whisper that not many men hear; to be on God's prospect list, to be on God's active list for inner working.

My fellow man, do something about it. Remember, a thousand men work where you work—and perhaps you are the only one that feels that tug. God yearns over them all, but they do not listen. They will not hear and they kill it within them.

If it is still alive and tugging at your heart, thank God, and follow the light—"Come every soul by sin oppressed, there's mercy with the Lord."

The Gift of
Eternal Life

*Even so must the Son of man be lifted up: That
whosoever believeth in him should not perish,
but have eternal life.* (John 3:14–15)

S ome things in our human lives are so basi-
cally unimportant that we never miss them if
we do not have them. Some other things, even
some that we just take for granted, are so important that if we do not grasp them and hold them
and secure them for all eternity, we will suffer ir-
reparable loss and anguish.

When we come to the question of our own relationship with God through the merits of our Lord
Jesus Christ, we come to one of those areas which
in a supreme degree is truly a matter of life and
death.

This is so desperately a matter of importance for every human being who comes into the world that I first become indignant, and then I become sad, when I try to give spiritual counsel to a person who looks me in the eye and tells me: "Well, I am trying to make up my mind if I should accept Christ or not."

Such a person gives absolutely no indication that he realizes he is talking about the most important decision he can make in his lifetime—a decision to get right with God, to believe in the eternal Son, the Savior, to become a disciple, an obedient witness to Jesus Christ as Lord.

How can any man or woman, lost and undone, sinful and wretched, alienated from God, stand there and intimate that the death and resurrection of Jesus Christ and God's revealed plan of salvation do not take priority over some of life's other decisions?

Now, the particular attitude revealed here about "accepting Christ" is wrong because it makes Christ stand hat-in-hand, somewhere outside the door, waiting on our human judgment.

We know about His divine Person, we know that He is the Lamb of God who suffered and died in our place. We know all about His credentials. Yet we let Him stand outside on the steps like some poor timid fellow who is hoping he can find a job.

We look Him over, then read a few more devotional verses, and ask: "What do you think, Mabel? Do you think we ought to accept Him? I really wonder if we should accept Him."

And so, in this view, our poor Lord Christ stands hat-in-hand, shifting from one foot to another looking for a job, wondering whether He will be accepted.

Meanwhile, there sits the proud Adamic sinner, rotten as the devil and filled with all manner of spiritual leprosy and cancer. But he is hesitating; he is judging whether or not he will accept Christ.

Putting off the Christ

Doesn't that proud human know that the Christ he is putting off is the Christ of God, the eternal Son who holds the worlds in His hands? Does he not know that Christ is the eternal Word, the Jesus who made the heavens and the earth and all things that are therein?

Why, this One who patiently waits for our human judgment is the One who holds the stars in His hands. He is the Savior and Lord and head over all things to the Church. It will be at His word that the graves shall give up their dead, and the dead shall come forth, alive forevermore. At His word, the fire shall burst loose and burn up the earth and the heavens and the stars and planets shall be swept away like a garment.

He is the One, the Mighty One!

And yet there He stands, while we animated clothespins—that's what we look like and that's what we are—decide whether we will accept Him or not. How grotesque can it be?

The question ought not to be whether I will accept Him; the question ought to be whether He will accept me!

But He does not make that a question. He has already told us that we do not have to worry or disturb our minds about that. "And him that cometh to me I will in no wise cast out" (John 6:37).

He has promised to receive us, poor and sinful though we be. But the idea that we can make Him stand while we render the verdict of whether He is worthy of our acceptance is a frightful calumny—and we ought to get rid of it!

Now, I think we should get back to our original premise that our relationship to Jesus Christ is a matter of life or death to us.

The average person with even a minimum of instruction in church or Sunday school will generally take two things for granted, without argument.

The first is that Jesus Christ came into the world to save sinners. That is declared specifically in the Bible, and it is declared in other words adding up to the same thing all through the New Testament.

If we have been reared in gospel churches, we also generally will take for granted the second fact: that we are saved by faith in Christ alone, without our works and without our merit.

I am discussing these two basic things with you here because too many individuals take them for granted, believe them to be true; and still they are asking, "How do I know that I have come into a saving relationship with Jesus Christ?" We had better find the answer because this is the matter of life or death.

The fact that Christ Jesus came into the world to save sinners is a matter of record. It needs no further proof. It is a fact—yet the world is not saved!

Right here in America, in our own neighborhoods, thousands and tens of thousands of people still are not saved.

Just the fact that He came to save sinners is not enough—that fact in itself cannot save us.

A friend or neighbor may tell us, "Well, I have gone to this certain church all my life. I have been confirmed, baptized and all the rest. I am going to take the chance that it will get me through."

My friend, your odds are not that good—you do not even have a chance. If your relation to Jesus Christ is not a saving relation, then you are on your own without a guide and without a compass. It is not a chance you have; it is suicide that you are committing. It is not a chance in 10 times 10,000. It is either be right or be dead; in this case, be right or be eternally lost.

There are millions all around us who have some Bible knowledge. They would tell you they have no argument with the fact that Jesus Christ came into the world to save sinners. They may even make a little joke about their own failures and shortcomings—they would not call them sins. They would likely excuse themselves from having to make a personal decision because they are not nearly as bad as Mr. Jones or Mrs. Smith down the street.

The point is that they may be able to recite John 3:16 or quote something nice about the whole world needing a Savior—and in an unusually tender moment there might be the sign of a tear in the eye. But they are lost. They are really far from God. They know that they are not converted because they have all known some person who had confessed Jesus Christ, been soundly converted and started living a transformed life.

Yes, they all know the difference. They know they are not converted, but they would rather not be told about the fate of the sinner when he dies.

Oh, that lost men and women would get concerned to the point of asking and finding out how they may come into a saving relationship with the Savior, Jesus Christ!

Three answers

Now, go to the average Christian brother, a converted man and probably a substitute teacher for the Bible class, and ask him: "How can I come into a saving relation to Jesus Christ so that it works for me?"

He will probably give you one of three answers, or he may give you all three answers. If you came to me, you would get the same, so this is not a criticism of anyone. This is simply a statement.

You would get the same answer from Billy Graham and you would get the same answer from the most isolated and unknown layman who has committed his way to Jesus Christ.

First you would be told that it is a matter of faith, that you must believe what God says about His Son, as in Acts 16:31: "Believe on the Lord Jesus Christ, and thou shalt be saved." That is the Bible answer that you would get.

Then, the person answering your question might add: "There is also the willingness to receive from God, as in John 1:12: 'But as many as received him . . . even to them that believe on his name.' "

So there in John's Gospel you find the close relationship in faith of believing and receiving.

But in our day, you will also be likely to get a third answer, and that is the one we are considering here. In all likelihood, if you would ask a number of Christian people how to come into this blessed saving relationship with Christ, someone is going to tell you: "Why, you just accept Christ!"

Let me say here that I do not want to make God responsible for anything I do, or anything I tell you. I have had my long talks with God and He knows how grateful and thankful I am if He can bless me and guide me and use me to do a few little things for Him. He surely knows that I am available as long as I am able to pray and think and speak a good word for Him, as long as I last.

What I am saying on this contemporary subject of "accepting Christ" is not a personal whim. Actually, I was kneeling by the little couch in my study upstairs, kneeling there with my Bible open, and I was engaged with God in doing a little repenting on my own accord—my own.

All of this came to me so clearly that I just wrote down a few notes, and said, "I am going to talk to the people about this." You are my friends, and I tell you that perhaps I am introducing some things here that God did not say to me, but maybe you will agree that you would rather hear a sermon from the outline the man got while on his knees than to know that he had gotten it somewhere else.

Well, that is it; a popular answer in our day is that we find Christ by accepting Him. You will find when I am through that I am not being critical. Probably our expressions in language do not always tell us what our hearts know.

Not found in the Bible

You may be surprised, as I was, when I ran this thing down and found that the expression "accept Christ" does not occur in the Bible. It is not found in the New Testament at all. I have looked it up in *Strong's Exhaustive Concordance,* and the old editors worked on that volume so long and so thoroughly that it does not skip a single word.

Strong's concordance shows very definitely that the word accept is never used in the Bible in the sense of our accepting God or accepting Jesus as our Savior.

It does seem strange that while we do not find its use anywhere in the Bible, the phrase, "Will you accept Christ?" or "Have you accepted Christ?" have become the catchwords throughout our soul-winning circles.

I am not trying to question our good intentions. I am sure that I have used this same expression many times—but still we have to admit that it does not occur in the Bible at all.

The words accept and acceptance are used in the Scriptures in a number of ways, but never in connection with believing on Christ or receiving Christ for salvation or being saved.

My concern in this matter is my feeling that "easy acceptance" has been fatal to millions of people who may have stopped short in matters of faith and obedience.

It is interesting to note that many groups of Christian workers and preachers and evangelists everywhere are calling for revival. Spiritual life in many areas seems to be in a low state and in many cases people are passing along the word about "prayer for revival."

But here is the odd thing: no one seems to stop and raise a question, such as: "Perhaps the reason we need revival so badly is the fact that we did not get started right in the first place."

This is why I have questioned the wide use of the soul-winning catchword, "Will you accept Christ? Just bow your head and accept Christ!"

I cannot estimate the number, although I think it is a very large number, of people who have been brought into some kind of religious experience by a fleeting formality of "accepting Christ," and a great, great number of them are still not saved. They have not been brought into a genuine saving relationship with Jesus Christ. We see the results all around us—they generally behave like religious sinners instead of like born-again believers.

That is why there is such a great stirring about the need for revival. That is why so many are asking, "What is the matter with us? We seem so dead, so lifeless, so apathetic about spiritual things!"

I say again that I have come to the conclusion that there are far too many among us who have thought that they accepted Christ—but nothing has come of it within their own lives and desires and habits. Will you just examine this matter a little more closely with me?

This kind of philosophy in soul winning, the idea that it is the easiest thing in the world to "accept Jesus," permits the man or woman to accept Christ by an impulse of the mind, or emotions. It allows us to gulp twice and sense an emotional feeling that may come over us, and then say, "I have accepted Christ."

All of you are aware of some of the very evident examples of the shortcomings in this approach to conversion and the new birth.

A Christian lady interested in the boys and girls goes out to the playground where several hundred children are engaged in their play and games. When she comes back, she reports with enthusiasm that she was able to persuade a group of about seventy children to stop their play and "accept Christ in their hearts."

An illustration

I actually was told of a group of preachers and laymen gathered in a hotel dining room and when the issue of soul-winning came up, one of the preachers said, "It is the easiest thing in the world, and I will give you a demonstration."

When the waiter came to his table, this brother said, "Can I have a minute of your time?"

The waiter said, "Yes, sir."

"Are you a Christian?" the preacher asked.

"No, sir. I am not a Christian."

"Wouldn't you like to be a Christian?"

"Well—well, I haven't thought too much about it."

"You know, all you have to do is accept Christ into your heart—will you accept Him?"

"Well, I guess so—yes, sir."

"All right, then, you just bow your head for a moment."

So, while the man who has been placed in a corner is thinking most about his tip, the soul-winner prays: "Now, Lord, here is a man who wants to accept You. And he takes You now as his Savior. Bless him real good. Amen!"

So, the waiter gets an enthusiastic handshake, and turns away to do his job, and he is just the same as when he came into the room.

But the demonstrating preacher turns to the group and says, "It is a simple matter. You can all see how easy it is to lead someone to Christ."

I think these are matters about which we must be legitimately honest and in which we must seek the discernment of the Holy Spirit. I hope that the waiter had better sense than the reverend because if he did not he is damned. These are things about which we cannot afford to be wrong. To be wrong is to still be lost and far from God. This is a matter of life or death and eternity.

When we are considering the importance to any human being of a right and saving relationship to Jesus Christ, we cannot afford to be wrong.

I think there is much abuse and that it is a great misconception to try to deal with men and women in this shallow manner when we know the great importance of conviction and concern and repentance when it comes to conversion, spiritual regeneration, being born from above by the Spirit of God.

It would be a healthy sign if the whole Church of Christ would rise up and ask God for fresh air in this matter; asking God for courage to consider and analyze where we stand in our efforts to win people to the Savior.

I am not trying to downgrade anybody in his or her efforts to win souls. I am just of the opinion that we are often too casual and there are too many tricks that can be used to make soul-winning encounters completely painless and at no cost and with no inconvenience.

Some people that we deal with on this "quick and easy" basis have such little preparation and are so ignorant of the plan of salvation that they would be willing to bow their heads and "accept" Buddha or Zoroaster or Father Divine if they thought that they could get rid of us in that way.

An Old Testament illustration

I think back to that time when God was dealing with the Israelites in bondage in Egypt. Suppose that Moses had said to the Israelites, "Do you accept the blood on the doorpost?"

They would have said, "Yes, of course. We accept the blood."

Moses then would have said, "That's fine. Now goodbye; I will be seeing you."

They would have stayed right in Egypt, slaves for the rest of their lives.

But their acceptance of the blood was a decision of action. Their acceptance of the blood of the Passover meant that they stayed awake all night; girded, ready, shoes on their feet, staffs in their hands, eating the food of the Passover, ready for the moving of God. Then, when the trumpet blasts sang sweet and clear, they all arose and started for the Red Sea. When they got to the Red Sea, having acted in faith, God was there to hold back the sea and they went out, never to return!

Their acceptance had the right kind of feet under it. Their acceptance gave them the guts to do something about it in the demonstration of their faith in God and His word.

Consider also the case of the prodigal son in the midst of the pigs with their dirt and filth and smell. Suppose you were concerned about him, about his own rags and his hunger.

"I have good news for you," you tell him. "Your father will forgive you if you will accept it. Will you accept it?"

He looks up from where he is reclining among the pigs, trying to keep warm, and replies: "Yeah, I'll accept it."

"Do you accept your father's reconciling and saving word?"

"Yes, I do!"

"That's fine. All right, goodbye. Hope to see you again."

You leave him in the pigpen. You leave him still in the dirt and filth. But that is not the way it happened in the story Jesus told in Luke 15.

The fellow was in there with the pigs and the filth—but something was stirring in his own heart and mind, and he said within himself: "If I am ever going to get out of this mess, I will have to make a decision. I must arise and go to my father."

I guess all of us know the next line:

"So he got up and went!"

Remember that?

"So he got up and went!"

Acceptance to the Jews meant strict obedience from that moment on. Acceptance to the prodigal son meant repentance in line with his acceptance.

I realize that the word accept has come close to being a synonym for the word receive. But I want to tell you what it means to accept Christ and then I want you to search your own heart and say, "Have I ever really accepted Christ? Do I accept Christ? Have I accepted Him at all?"

I want to give you a definition for accepting Christ. To accept Christ in anything like a saving relation is to have an attachment to the person of Christ that is revolutionary, complete and exclusive.

What I am talking about is an attachment to the person of Christ, and that is so important. It is something more than getting in with a crowd that you like. It is something more than the social fellowship of some nice fellow that gives you a thrill when you touch his hand. It is something more than getting in with a group that puts on their uniforms and plays softball together on Tuesday evenings.

Those things are all harmless enough, God knows. But accepting Jesus Christ is more than finding association with a group you like. It is not just going on a picnic or taking a hike. We have those activities in our church and I believe in them. But they are not the things that are as important as your acceptance of Jesus Christ. The answer you are seeking in Jesus Christ does not mean that you are just getting in with a religious group who may not be any better off than you are.

Accepting Jesus Christ, receiving Jesus Christ into your life means that you have made an attachment to the person of Christ that is revolutionary in that it reverses the life and transforms it completely.

It is an attachment to the person of Christ. It is complete in that it leaves no part of the life unaffected. It exempts no area of the life of the total man; his total being.

This kind of an attachment to the person of Christ means that Christ is not just one of several interests. It means that He is the one exclusive attachment as the sun is the exclusive attachment of the earth. As the earth revolves around the sun, and the sun is its center and the core of its being, so Jesus Christ is the Son of righteousness, and to become a Christian by the grace of God means to come into His orbit and begin to revolve around Him exclusively.

In the sense of spiritual life and desire and devotion, it means to revolve around Him completely, exclusively—not partly around Him.

This does not mean that we do not have other relationships—we all do because we all live in a complex world. You give your heart to Jesus. He becomes the center of your transformed life. But you may be a man with a family. You are a citizen of the country. You have a job and an employer. In the very nature of things, you have other relationships. But by faith and through grace, you have now formed an exclusive relationship with your Savior, Jesus Christ. All of your other relationships are now conditioned and determined by your one relationship to Jesus Christ, the Lord.

Jesus laid down the terms of Christian discipleship and there have been people who have criticized and said, "Those words of Jesus sound harsh and cruel." His words were plain and He was saying to every one of us: "If you have other relationships in life which are more important and more exclusive than your spiritual relationship to the eternal Savior, then you are not my disciple."

First and last and all

To accept Christ, then, is to attach ourselves to His holy person; to live or die, forever. He must be first and last and all. All of our other relationships are conditioned and determined and colored by our one exclusive relation to Him.

To accept Christ without reservation is to accept His friends as your friends from that moment on.

If you find yourself in an area where Christ has no friends, you will be friendless except for the one Friend who sticketh closer than a brother.

It means that you will not compromise your life. You will neither compromise your talk nor your habits of life.

We have to confess that we find there are people who are such cowards that when they are with a crowd that denies the Son of God and disgraces the holy name of Jesus, they allow themselves to be carried away in that direction. Are they Christians? You will have to answer that.

A Christian is one who has accepted Jesus' friends as his friends and Jesus' enemies as his enemies by an exclusive attachment to the person of Christ.

I made up my mind a long time ago. Those who declare themselves enemies of Jesus Christ must look upon me as their enemy—and I ask no quarter from them. And if they are the friends of Jesus Christ they are my friends and I do not care what color they are or what denomination they belong to.

To accept the Lord means to accept His ways as our ways. We have taken His Word and His teachings as the guide in our lives. To accept Christ means that I accept His rejection as my rejection. When I accept Him I knowingly and willingly accept His cross as my cross. I accept His life as my life—back from the dead I come and up into a different kind of life. It means that I accept His future as my future.

I am talking about the necessity of an exclusive attachment to His person—that is what it means to accept Christ. If the preachers would tell people what it actually means to accept Christ and receive Him and obey Him and live for Him we would have fewer converts but those who would come and commit would not backslide and founder. They would stick.

Actually, preachers and ministers of the gospel of Christ should remember that they are going to stand before the judgment seat of Christ, and they will have to tell a holy Savior why they betrayed His people in this way.

Now, please do not go out and tell people that Mr. Tozer says you should never use those words, "accept Christ." I have tried to make it plain that we should always invite those who are not Christians to come to Jesus, to believe what God says about the Savior, to receive Him by faith into their lives and to obey Him; and to accept Christ as their Savior if they know what it means—an exclusive attachment to the person of Christ.

Are you aware that many of the great preachers and the great evangelists who have touched the world, including such men as Edwards and Finney in the past, have declared that the church is being betrayed by those who insist on Christianity being made too easy. Oh, what a host of people have been betrayed into thinking that they were converted when all that they did was to join a religious group.

I would say frankly that moral sanity requires that we settle this important matter first of all, settling our personal and saving relationship with God. The way some of us live, we ought not to be surprised when some concerned friend or brother asks, "Are we Christians, indeed?"

In some Christian groups, the believers actually make fun and laugh at Christians in other groups who occasionally arise and sing the words of an old hymn: "Do I love the Lord, or no?"

No serious-minded person should ever laugh at any other man or woman standing under the wide expanse of heaven with death only three jumps ahead and who is contemplating: "My God, do I really love You or not? Have I been mistaken in a meaningless religious connection? My God, what must I do to be saved?"

Many of us better start asking questions today. We know that we had better not try to stand on our own reputation.

There is nothing in the whole world of more value and of greater meaning than to come back into the family of God by faith and through His grace. There is no joy compared to that which God gives us when He forgives us, cleanses us, re-stores and saves us, and assures us that the gift of God is indeed eternal life, to as many as will believe!

Other Titles by A.W. Tozer:

7/9/11

10/11/ 11

3/9/18
_____

9/3/20